DIARY OF AN OBSESSION

Colin Plumb

FOREWORD

I am so pleased to say that the proceeds of the sale of this book will go to the British Heart Foundation and the Cancer Research Foundation, 50% to each. The BHF and cancer funds are very close to my heart and no more so because they have not only helped me, but also my mother and father in law, god bless them.

The St. Nicholas Hospice in Bury St Edmunds also cared for my father in the last weeks of his life, such wonderful, lovely professional people, they cared for my father lovingly. I certainly will never forget them, absolute ANGELS all of them.

This book is dedicated to every Ipswich Town fan not just in Suffolk, East Anglia, but in every corner of the whole UK, also Europe and the rest of the world. These days we have fans everywhere, it's so good to see, so wherever you are, be it in dear old Bury St Edmunds or in sunny Australia, I do hope you have enjoyed my first book about our club Ipswich Town, let's just lastly all hope that with our fantastic new owners, lovely chairman and very hard working CEO and manager we finally get back to where we should be and that CERTAINLY IS NOT THE 3RD DIVISION of the football league!

Finally, thank you to Ipswich Town Football Club for the cover image, an ariel shot of my spiritual home Portman Road and to James Hobson (https://www.JamesJamesJames.co.uk) for retouching the photograph for me.

All the best

Colin

x

Colin pictured here with his elder brother John and loving mother Joan

TALKING TOWN PODCAST

Given Colin shares a birthday with Sir Bobby Robson, it seems appropriate to paraphrase a quote from one of English football's greatest managers

"What is a club in any case? It's the noise, the passion, the feeling of belonging, the pride."

And that's exactly what we wanted to bring to the table with Talking Town.

When lockdown hit in 2020 it put a lid on everyday life and all the things we take for granted.

Football was gone but we could still pick up a mic and talk on the internet about the one thing we all have in common, Ipswich Town FC.

One of our first attempts ended up with zero views, we'd forgotten to press the "go live" button!

But from there our audience began to grow and blossom into the community that it is today.

And that's how we first met Colin Plumb.

He'd referenced Talking Town on the BBC Suffolk post-match phone-in a few times and then started contributing to our shows on YouTube.

We often talk about sliding door moments on the show and Colin and Matt Stannard's friendship is another for that list.

Had they not met through the Talking Town community then you probably wouldn't be holding this book in your hand right now.

We're always amazed at how Talking Town has impacted people across the globe, Tractor Boys and Girls tuning in from Australia to Botswana, blue and white in their DNA.

Enjoy this journey through Ipswich Town history, of lifting trophies, European adventures, and brilliant players.

Let's hope that our great football club can return to those days and give future generations something to write about in the years to come.

Martin Lambert
Rich Moss
Matt Phillips

Ollie Moss, Richard Moss, Matt Phillips, Martin Lambert, Archie Moss and Colin – Talking Town at Bury Town Football Club

INTRODUCTION

Before you embark on reading about Colin's (and many of our own) obsession, a few words from me, Matt Stannard. Colin is a very good friend of mine and when he approached me to help him share his diary, I of course was only too pleased to help. Little did I know it was well over 200 pages of handwritten manuscript that needed typing up - so I do apologise now if there is anything that has been typed incorrectly.

As a tractor boy myself and not being old enough to have experienced the glory days of Ipswich, I thoroughly enjoyed being the first person to read the diary as I typed it up and I felt myself becoming immersed in the emotions of what it must have been like to have grown up with an Ipswich of old, and what it was like to be FA Cup winners and bask in European glory.

In my opinion Colin has done an amazing job of capturing what it means to be an Ipswich Town supporter and you can't help but connect with the highs that we all still get today, as well as the lows. Colin captures the emotion so eloquently and, in my view, he is a real tribute to Ipswich Town fans across the globe.

I hope you enjoy reading it as much as I did and thank you!

Take care and of course **Come On You Blues**!!!

Matt

1 - THE BEGINNING (1964 - 1965)

To be quite honest I cannot remember too much about my first season of supporting the Super Blues, but what I can remember especially is my very first game which was against Coventry City at home and we lost 1-3, Blackwood scoring the goal I remember.

We didn't go to so many games in the early days as it probably was a question of finance for my dad as he was a truly working class man on working class wages, but when we could go me, John and dad we most certainly did.

1964-1965 season was probably remembered more for the awful start we had not winning in our first nine games in the league but we were able to pick up and finished a creditable fifth in the Division 2 table.

My first win was against Newcastle at home, we won 3-1 and Brogan and Hegan (2) scored the goals, two players who were to become heroes of mine. That season we beat Portsmouth 7-0 at home with Frank Brogan scoring a hat trick.

My first derby win was on January 2nd 1965 when we beat Norwich City 3-0 with the great Gerry Baker scoring twice and Joe Broadfoot netting the other, great memories. I used to love the atmosphere of a local derby and I still do, 100%. We ended the season by beating Crystal Palace 3-2 at home with Baker, Broadfoot and Baxter scoring, the end of my first season of what was to become a fantastic love affair with Ipswich Town FC. Baker finished top scorer with 16 goals, Brogan had the most appearances with 43.

2 - THE 1965 - 1966 SEASON

This season started off with a home game against what were the great Preston North End - we won 1-0 and the scorer was none other than Gerry Baker., a great goal scorer of the time at Portman Road.

Myself and Dad were still only going to a handful of games a season and I always remember going on the train from Bury St. Edmunds station and the platform was always packed with fans going to the games, lovely memories indeed.

We lost at Carrow Road this season 0-1 as we did the previous season, that was 1-2, not a great start to my Carrow Road memories, but they would get extremely better in the years to come, more on that later in the story. We did AGAIN beat Norwich City at home this time it was 2-0 and the great Ray Crawford and a Baxter penalty sealed the points in front of a 22,690 crowd at Portman Road.

Manchester city won the second division that season and we finished a disappointing 15th in the table which was quite sad as we had a very good season in 1964-1965. We finished that season at home with a great 5-2 win over Wolves with Crawford 2, Baker, Hegan and Hawkins (O.G.) scoring the goals to end our season with at least a win and send us all home happy on the train to Bury St Edmunds with 2 points. As it was then, it was 2 points for a win, 1 point for a draw.

Baker was again top scorer with 15 goals and Billy Baxter was top of the appearances with 49. At least we now had Ray Crawford back at the club and what a difference he made in the following season to come, welcome back TO YOUR CLUB RAY a true Ipswich Town legend.

3 - THE 1966 - 1967 SEASON

England had just won the World Cup at Wembley beating West Germany 4-2 A.E.T and everyone was so excited about the season ahead all over the country.

The first game of the season that year was against Huddersfield Town, we won 3-0 with goals from Baker, Spearitt and Brogan, by the way Brogan and Baker had two famous brothers, Jim Brogan of Celtic and Joe Baker who played for Arsenal at Highbury), that game against Huddersfield I remember really well as all or most small children were allowed to sit on the perimeter of the pitch in these days, fantastic views of the game they were from pitch level superb!!! I was 9 years old at the time and 13,570 gates used to feel like 50,000 to me at that time when I was a child.

The season had got off and running and my first job on a Sunday morning was to go and get the News of the World paper for my dad and it was a regular scrap when I first got home to be the first one to read the report , something I normally won because generally I was always the person to go and get the paper and would read it on my way home, I loved seeing where we were in the table. My first few seasons we hardly went to away games as it was far too expensive for my dad, especially with two boys as well to take to games, it was to change in later seasons, that was for sure 100%.

One game that stuck out that season was the F.A. Cup 5th Round replay against the superb Manchester City of the time, we had drawn at Maine Road 1-1 and forced a replay at Portman Road, there was 47,000 at Maine Road and 30,155 at Portman Road for the replay.

Dad passed me and John down to the front so we could both see the game, it was done all the time in the 60's at all grounds in England. My mum even came to that game, a real novelty as she hardly ever came to games!!

Another memory of the 66-67 season was a 6-1 over Northampton Town. Brogan got a hat-trick with two of those coming from the penalty spot, he was a brilliant penalty taker, Frank was always so ice cool at putting away penalties.

Later that season another hat-trick was to follow and on that day in March 1967 my hero for quite a few seasons was born, his name was Colin Viljoen, a midfield player from South Africa. He was making his debut against Portsmouth at home and scored three of the four goals in a 4-2 win, a game I have never forgotten to this day.

After all of this my first full season was drawing to a close, we played the eventual champions of 66-67 on the last day who were Coventry City the game ended 1-1 and my new idol Viljoen got the goal, a super end to what had been a super season with Town finishing 5th, eight points behind Wolves and nine points behind Coventry not a bad start for the fresh faced youngster from Bury St Edmunds who had just witnessed his third season of the football league.

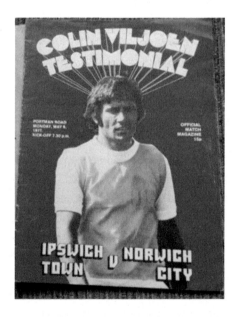

Colin Viljoen (pictured here on Testimonial Program from 1977)

4 - CHAMPIONS AGAIN - 1967-1968

The summer seemed to go on and on forever, the only thing that I wanted, was to see those players jogging out onto the hallowed turf and get on with it again. But as sure as eggs are eggs the inevitable holiday break in Yarmouth with my mum, dad and brother and no end of kicking footballs with my mate Kev up the car park at least got me through what seemed to be an eternity, but got through it I did and before I knew it we would be kicking off another 2nd division season against Middlesbrough at Ayresome Park.

Now, the season before had been promising, and my dad, the eternal optimist kept saying to me and my brother that before long we would be back to the 1st division, something that I for one had never seen, unlike my lucky brother and dad who had witnessed that unbelievable season back in 1961-1962 when we won the league title. Middlesbrough away first game, never an easy place to go but Town went there and won 2-0, two points, we were up and running, this was quickly followed by another away game at Blackpool which finished 0-0 a good point at the seaside nonetheless and we had secured three points out of four and we still hadn't played on the hallowed turf yet, maybe just maybe Dad was to be proved right and I might have a chance to see top flight football for the first time of my life, time would certainly tell that was for sure.

By this time things had changed a little as Dad now was the proud owner of a Wolsey 1500 a car he was almost as dedicated to as a he was his beloved Ipswich Town, but what a difference it made no more waiting on cold platforms in December, no we were to be made to feel like royalty, going to football in a car, unheard of at that time of day, but this was reality and enjoy it we certainly did. Our first home game in the 67-68 season was against Bristol City and after a good start to the season we carried it on with an impressive 5-0 win, of which Brogan scored another hat trick. He and my new idol Viljoen scored. We went home in the car talking all the time like supporters do in August about what might be at the end of the season and after 5 points out of 6 we certainly were not talking relegation, that was for sure.

We never had a big squad in those days, but what we did have was a squad that would more times than not pull together in a crisis, something that come the end of the season would hold them in very good stead indeed. The squad was to be strengthened later on in the season with the signing of Peter Morris and John O'Rouke, what a double signing those proved to be for Bill McGarry, more about that later.

The games came and went, and by the time we had got to the beginning of November we had still only lost one game and that was to Blackburn away, a very impressive start indeed. I could sense something special was going to happen that season because every time we went to the games it was just as if it was meant to be, people standing next to you were always happy, merrily spinning their rattles and singing their heart's out for a team full of spirit and endeavour. December was upon us before we knew where we were and it was to prove our most disappointing part of the season, we played QPR away followed by Portsmouth and Middlesbrough at home and we lost all three games, not a very good way to start your Christmas, but at least we were to get it out of our systems relatively early on and come back strong in the later part of the season, something we surely did.

My dad kept saying to me and my brother, don't worry lad's all teams go through a bad spell and good teams come out of it. He was to be proved very right at the end of the season.
 We stopped the slump with a decent point away at Bristol City, a goal from Billy Baxter "now there's a novelty" but a point and Town were back on track. We were playing well again and picked up points almost everywhere, and this was to be the season that Dad took me to my first away game, Norwich City at Carrow Road no less. Now these were the days like I tried to explain earlier when working class people didn't earn a king's ransom and because of that, something I didn't understand then, but certainly do now, away games were very much a luxury. But go we did and we set

off quite early, stopping two or three times along the way for a sandwich and a cup of coffee. Norwich away in the 60's was like going to Newcastle today such was the state of the roads. Anyway get there we did and the first thing I can remember was seeing so many people wearing green and yellow, something I obviously was not very used to having only been to home games, but not to worry because there was still a very large amount of Town fans there because of it being a local derby and that made a ten year old feel a whole lot better. The game itself was to prove a cracker and Town went on to win a superb game 4-3 with my hero Colin Viljoen scoring a hat-trick, what a game to collect the match ball in front of 30,022 screaming fans. After the game we made our way back to the car amongst several delirious Ipswich fans, the journey home did not seem half as long as we had defeated the enemy and kept our promotion hopes alive thanks to Viljoen and Houghton. We all talked endlessly about promotion and maybe the chance to see the likes of Best, Moore and the like at Portman Road the following season, something that really was becoming more of a reality as each week and game passed us by.

With 15 or so games to go McGarry decided to plunge into the transfer market and in came John O'Rourke and Peter "Diesel" Morris, two superb signings indeed they were to really make their mark as Town went in search of first division status big time. O'Rourke made an immediate impact scoring twice against Cardiff at home making him an instant hero with the North Stand faithful, Morris with his never say die attitude in midfield was also a big hit with the Town fans. O'Rourke and the superb Crawford really hit it off and in the last 15 games of the season scored 21 goals between them as Town went relentlessly in pursuit of the title. One of the most important games of the run in was to be an encounter with QPR at Portman Road a game I still remember vividly because of if nothing else the arrogance of a very young Rodney Marsh taking a penalty up the Churchmans End. He seemed to take about a mile long run up and place the kick past an amazed Ken Hancock. QPR were a good side that season and it was neck and neck with Town all season as to who would eventually win the title, fortunately the 2-2 draw with Rangers kept us right in there and the atmosphere from a 28,000 crowd that day was truly amazing, a great day out. Palace away, followed by Pompey away were always going to be difficult games in the run in but superb displays by the Town and the goalscoring form of Crawford and O'Rourke meant that four points were secured and meant we only needed a point from the last game at home to Blackburn for the title, what a season, and how myself, my dad and my brother looked forward to May 11th, the last game of the season. May 4th to May 11th seemed to take forever, but arrive it did and I can remember my dad saying we'll be going early on Saturday boy's to take in some of the atmosphere. I'm glad we did. It was an unbelievable day. We left home at about 11am arriving at Ipswich by car at 12:15pm, the A45 as it was known then wasn't the A14 as it is now believe me. We used to have to go through all the little towns and villages in those days, not like it is now being dual carriageway all the way and taking about 30 minutes, my what a different world it is today. Anyway we arrived at Portman Road at about 12:30pm after a 15 minute walk from where my dad used to always park his car, quite a way from the ground because like I said before Dad loved that car and didn't want it damaged or the like so he kept it well away, a good policy to have. When we got into the ground on the North Stand terrace at about 12:45pm the atmosphere was already brilliant with everybody full of hope that we would get the point we needed. No worries Ray Crawford scored the goal in front of the North Stand end to secure the point we needed in a 1-1 draw and then the party really started. As soon as the whistle went thousands of Town fans were flocking onto the super Ipswich pitch, something I'm sure the groundsman was not too happy with but again something I'm sure for once he would surely understand. The whole pitch was covered with fans baying for the likes of Baxter, Crawford, Viljoen and McGarry. They did salute the fans in the end, I remember them coming into the old tannoy box above where the players came out and the players and management thanked the fans over the public address system. Another thing I remember from that famous Saturday afternoon in May was the playing of Congratulations, that famous song of the 60s by Cliff Richard, it played and played and played again, but no one cared because promotion had been achieved. Eventually when we did get out of the ground and walked back to the car I remember saying to my dad "dad I'm actually going to see Best, Law and Charlton next season". Dad replied "Yes son, and also Moore, Hurst and Peters". I couldn't really believe it had happened and my dream of watching 1st Division football was real, very real indeed.

Ray Crawford – Middle Front Row (alongside Ted Philips) pictured here in the 61-62 winning side, fantastic in the 67-68 season.

Ray Crawford – England International

5 - BOBBY WHO? - 1968-1969

After everything that had gone before, the euphoria of promotion and the celebrations that followed, open top bus around Ipswich and champagne flowing, it was now time for everybody to take stock, fans included and get down to what would be a very hard season ahead and everyone knew it.

Bill McGarry and his staff had worked hard pre-season and all of this seemed to have paid off when Wolves were beaten 1-0 on a boiling Saturday afternoon in August. Now like I have said before and I don't mind repeating myself about close-seasons, they are alright if you are big time into tennis or cricket, but at the time, unlike the present day all I ever lived for was going to Portman Road with dad and John, none more than now as I was to embark on my first season of top class football. That first game at home to Wolves will always live in my memory because it was my first, first division game and I was so excited about it, especially the week before hand as it seemed like a year to come round.

But as with any day of the week Saturday 10th August 1968 did arrive and just as for any other game we set off about 11:30am to get to the ground at about 12:45pm. The main reason for that was not so much parking because you could more or less park where you wanted in those days it was more to do with match day queuing, you could sometimes stand waiting for up to an hour and a half just to get in. This was due mainly in those days because not many people were season ticket holders, so most people paid cash on the day at the turn style, hence the delays. Wolves in those days was a big game and for me to see those players in the old gold come out at our ground was heaven itself. Nearly 26,000 turned up for the first game and after being 0-0 at half time John O'Rourke our darling number 10 scored to give us the points, oh what joy, we had won my first, division one game. Going home that hot August evening I can still hear dad saying "that's a good win lads, but all the hard work has really yet to start", how right he was.

Every game in this division was eagerly awaited and the next two, away to Sunderland lost 0-3 and away to Leicester where we won 3-1 were two points gained, and not a bad start to the season, we had played 3 and had 4 points, my god, I as a 11 year old was starting to think about what John and Dad had witnessed in 1961-1962, how wrong I was to be.

The very next game was the kind that sticks in my memory, it was the first time I had had the chance to see the then mighty Leeds United, Brenner, Giles, Charlton & Co. Over 30,000 were in the ground that night and to see all those stars in lily white shirts on my ground was brilliant, we lost 3-2in what was a storming game but the real winners were the fans, it really was a superb game under the lights.

The next five games of our first season were to prove difficult, only one win against QPR 3-0 and things were starting to look a whole lot different than they did on that sunny afternoon in August when we beat Wolves. Only two more wins against Stoke at home 3-1 and Nottingham Forest away 2-1 by the end of October meant that McGarry had had enough and he left to join Wolves and Cyril Lea who had been a player for Town earlier in his career took over as caretaker-manager. Now dad and I liked Lea but it was always the intentions of the Cobbolds to get another manager.

Results really didn't improve dramatically but weren't too bad, but even so I never really thought he would get the job. Billy Bingham applied for the job as did Frank O'Farrell but the person the board turned to eventually was a 35 year old a rather lean looking man who had just been sacked by Fulham, his name Bobby Robson, now of course Sir Bobby Robson and my oh my what an introduction he was to get from certain members of the playing staff later on in his managerial career. Now that decision had been made by Cobbold and the board, we all had to get to grips with who this Bobby Robson was, it was okay for my dad and his generation because he had heard of him before, but to myself and the rest of my friends at school we hadn't got the foggiest who he was.

All my dad had told me was that he had been a very good wing-half (that's what they called them in the 60's) with West Bromwich Albion and Fulham and that he had won several caps for England, including playing in the famous 9-3 win over Scotland at Wembley.

I spoke to Steedy (Jon Steed) a very good friend of mine at school, and still is to this day, about Robson but like me he didn't know much about him, only that he was young, ambitious and wanted to put the Fulham thing behind him. Jon had been a great friend to myself ever since we started school at St. Johns in Bury, followed by St. Edmundsbury also in Bury St. Edmunds and then on to Silver Jubilee, where we were at the time of Robsons managerial baptism of fire. Whilst at the Jubilee school we used to do the same old school boy things like swap stickers in the playground and occasionally when your dad could afford it, show your mates some programmes that you had collected from previous games.

Now, Robson made his first step on the Ipswich ladder at Goodison Park against Everton a team full of international stars like Ball, Hervey, Kendall and Royle and the Town didn't let him down drawing 2-2- with the brilliant Crawford netting twice in front of 41,000 fanatical scousers, not a bad start to your managerial career. I can remember saying to dad that if we carry on like this you never know, I think we will stay up and Mr Robson might prove to be a good choice, how right I was going to be proved in the coming months and years, a legend was just about being born.

Another unusual thing about Robson was that he looked just like my father, a double if you like, he really did and as the years went on and we all got older the likeness between the two got even more, a fact I still relate to today even though Robson is grey and my father is now not with us.

After the Everton game we were all looking forward to welcoming Robson to Portman Road and this was to be on February 1st 1969 a home game against Manchester United no less. Now as I said before when we got promoted, to see Law, Charlton and especially

Best on the hallowed turf takes some believing but it was just about to happen. We left especially early for the game to get parked because dad knew there would be a big gate he couldn't have been more correct as 30,837 turned up to see Mr Robson and Bests debut at Portman Road. The atmosphere was special and the police allowed children to sit on the side of the pitch, something that I done with dads assistance to get over the wall and here I was 3 yards away from George Best, I couldn't believe it but it was true. Town played well and kept the potent strike force of Law, Best and Charlton at bay and went on to record Robsons first win with a 1-0 win an own goal from Tony Dunne, thanks Tony, we owe ya mate! Robson had really arrived and he was to really sort the place out in the coming months and years, a job he didn't mind doing and from the outside looking in, didn't mind who he told off or who he dropped, the sign of an excellent manager and person.

Games came and went during the coming months and a defeat at mighty Leeds was no disgrace, followed by a brilliant 2-0 win at Highbury against Arsenal, goals again from O'Rourke and Crawford. The last 12 games of the season saw Robson stamp his name on the job big time as Town went on a superb run of only 2 defeats and 15 points gained a really superb effort from a team just promoted and dead certs to go down with many people, me, my dad and brother not included I may say.

Towards the end of the season, Robson made some critical decisions as regards to the playing staff, Crawford left to join Charlton, Hancock left for Spurs, replaced by David Best in goal and Danny Hegan left to join WBA a move I for one was to grow to like as it brought Ian Collard the other way, a player I really admired later on in his career. Town finished the season 12th a great effort from all concerned and a great first season in the first division.

6 - HANG IN THERE BOYS - 1969-1970

Another summer had almost passed us by with Town not very active in the transfer market, that was to change as the season went on and with a great effect on where we were to eventually finish in the league and of course our first division status. The school holidays were great with a lot of football being played up the car park and down the famous pit in Bury St. Edmunds, but all I really wanted to be doing was going to see my beloved blues with Dad and John, a season which was to be kicked off with a first game against Nottingham Forest at home which was to be a quite lacklustre affair that ended 0-0.We all went with great expectations following the previous season, but with only 19,000 present we were to witness, which proved at the end of the season to be a season of struggle and Robsons first big test.

The next six games went by against Derby, Chelsea, incredibly Derby again, Coventry, Southampton and Spurs and only one point had been picked up all season, a nightmare of a start of which myself and Steedy were being ribbed big time at the Jubilee by so called Manchester United, Chelsea and Arsenal fans. Town are going down this year they kept saying, myself and Steedy kept a stiff upper lip and didn't let it show too much but boy deep down we were hurting, very much indeed in my case. Town meant everything to me and when we eventually got that first win of the season against Newcastle United at home it was as if a great weight had been lifted off my shoulders, goals from Ron Wigg and John O'Rourke meant I could eventually face them at school with my head held high. Dad kept saying to me and my brother don't worry we will be okay but like I've said before my dad was ever the optimistic and believe me at that time of following the Blues you had to be. The next eleven games of the season saw us win only two games and draw five, not bad, but after the poor start to the season things were not looking rosy at all. John O'Rourke decided to leave the club for Coventry City a decision that at the time had a devastating effect on me because I like so many other town fans had taken John to our hearts and also because Crawford had gone, I wondered when and where the next goal would come from.

Anyway, Robson went out and signed Mick Hill from Sheffield United, neither I nor my dad knew that much about him but he was to prove not to be too bad a player. Although Hill scored twice against Palace we were very much on a downward spiral and a shocking 4-1 defeat at home to Chelsea was to see us really hit rock bottom. Results just were not coming and fans at the ground were getting restless, I felt for Robson because everybody knew about the dressing room goings on early season, and all the talk early season about pay rises were not helping the cause at all. My idol Viljoen was one of those and I didn't really like what he said to Robson but I soon forgave him, he was after all my idol, Towns number 8 who scored that famous hat trick at Norwich City bless him. January came and another one of those players I was brought up with was to depart, Frank Brogan was leaving to sign for Halifax Town, Frank was one of those old fashioned wingers, hugged the touchline and loved to cut in and have a shot, a very good penalty taker as well, we would all miss him but time had told on Frank and it was time for a move on.

January was FA Cup time and since I had been supporting Town since 1964 apart from that game against Man City we always had got knocked out in round 3, this season was to be no different. We had been drawn at home to Manchester United, not a favourable draw, but Man Utd nonetheless which meant another chance to see Best and the boys. Now like everything else to do with Man Utd they do give you a chance because of their attacking style, so off me and my dad went along with 29,500 others hoping this would maybe be the season we have a bit of a run, how wrong we were! We got there early as usual, you had too in those days because the ground was busting with 30,000 inside. We went into the Churchmans for this game as the North Stand was full about 2 hours before kick off. We got quite a nice spot at the front near the wall and were eagerly awaiting the boys to come out. The Town played decent on the day and had several decent chances to win the game, but as a replay at old Trafford look inevitable Mick McNeil was to put through his own goal in the 90th minute, I couldn't believe it, absolutely devastated, going home in the car nobody spoke all the way home, another defeat in round three and only a relegation battle to look forward to.

After the cup defeat and a whole lot of mickey taking at school from so called mates it was back to what was fast becoming a disastrous season, we must hang in there boys I kept saying to Steedy and my dad at home. The next eight league games saw us only draw 3 and lose 5, my christ we were in trouble and I was getting more and more worried as time went on. Something had to happen and it did, Robson went out and signed two players who were to completely change our season, one was Jimmy Robertson a superb winger from Arsenal and the other was Frank Clarke from QPR a very decent centre forward the brother of Leeds Utd Allan Clarke.

There were seven games to go when they signed and relegation staring us in the face, but after a 2-0 win against Sunderland at home followed by a 2-0 defeat at Anfield, the rest of the season from my point of view was brilliant. Clarke & Robertson had really put some spark back into the squad and put smiles on peoples faces again in the crowd with their attitude towards helping the team survive. After a 1-1 draw at Palace in which Charlie Woods scored his final goal before leaving for Watford, next up were Arsenal at Portman Road, a game I shall never forget. It was a night game under the lights, something I always loved and still do, 25,000 at the ground and a superb atmosphere. Jimmy and Frank had really given us all hope but against Arsenal things started not so well with the Gunners going in front, but not to worry, what with the crowds help and boy it was deafening on the night the boys turned it round and won 2-1 with goals from Baxter and Clarke, a brilliant two points and we went home with a certain amount of hope that we could pull it round.

The last three games of the season were to prove essential in Robsons building of the club as First Division status was absolutely vital. Southampton were next up at Portman Road and Town won 2-0 with goals from Robertson and a Carroll penalty. We could all start resting easy as the master stroke that Mr Robson had supplied with the two signings was a brilliant piece of management on his part. A defeat at Nottingham Forest, 1-0, didn't really matter and as we went into the last game of the season against cup finalists Leeds Utd in a very good frame of mind. The last game against Leeds was a night game and Leeds had several players out due to the fact they had a cup final coming up against Chelsea. Nonetheless Town took the bull by its horns and turned Leeds over 3-2 with goals from Robertson (2) and Clarke a fitting way for those two to end the season and give us 18th place in the league and a little piece of respectability.

Another season had come to a close and we drove home with everybody happy that we had kept our first division status and all looking forward to the next season, what would that bring, who knows, who cares, we had hung in there.

7 - MIDLANDS BOUND - 1970-1971

Now at 13 years old, and feeling a bit of a big boy because I had just got into my teens, football had really started to take a hold of my life. I used to read anything to do with my obsession be it Goal, Shoot, the "Green Un" and most importantly the Sunday newspaper. I loved reading the reports on a Sunday morning in the News of the World. Somethings at thirteen have to take a back seat in life, like silly childish girls who only want a sneaky kiss in the corner of the playground or up the car park behind a high wall, what ever are they like, all I wanted to do was get my football out with my friend Key Gaught or even more importantly get over with my dad to see, in my eyes the best football team in the world, apart maybe from that average Brazil side at the time, what was that blokes name Pele or someone, I would have Colin Viljoen anytime he was my idol.

Season 1970-1971 would start at Stoke City's Victoria Ground, quite ironic actually because that was to become later in the season the very first ground I had visited to see an away FA Cup tie, more on that expedition later on in the chapter. Stoke City in the 70s were not a bad side and so a 0-0 draw on the opening day seemed very acceptable, certainly myself and dad thought so, a point away was always a good result in Division 1. I talked so much during pre-season to Dad about the struggle we had most of last season but dad being dad just said "don't worry son, we will be alright this season no problem" he always talked Town up, never down, and hated anybody else talking them down, just like me now, I detest people who talk them down, after all they are our local club aren't they apart from Bury Town F.C that is and they won't be in Division 1 while I'm around I know, bless 'em.

Coventry at home after Stoke was a real disappointment, we set off thinking that we we were to improve on last season but a 2-0 home defeat in front of 21,000 was a real kick in the gooleys, this was followed four days later by another home game against Nottingham Forest, again, no goals for Town but at least we got a draw out of it and two points were secured out of six, not brilliant but at least we hadn't been beaten in two of the three games. Mind you what was really worrying myself and dad was the fact we just weren't scoring, a big worry for any football fan at the start of the season.

My first real away game was to come next, a trip to Derby County, now we hadn't really planned it before the season started but I think Dad thought it was about time to embark on an away day trip. Derby County were starting to become a real force in English football with players like Mackay, Hector and McFarland, so to go to the Baseball Ground was going to be out of this word for me. The journey itself took about four hours, because like I said before the roads were not brilliant in those days and we must have stopped about three times for tea and sandwich breaks. Dad did love his flask, he loved a flask of tea and a good old fashioned cheese sarnie, so did I and we would always have enough, that's what my mum was like, if you wanted a pack up of four sarnies she would make you six, bless her. Anyway, after what had seemed a lifetime we arrived in Derby, a shock for the average lad from Suffolk because I don't think I'd ever seen so many terrace houses and industrial chimneys in my life. We parked in one of the back streets near the ground. Now the Baseball Ground isn't the biggest in the world, but it was very noisy inside with nearly 31,000 inside it was a bit intimidating for one so young, but I soon got used to it and felt so happy because I really was watching my team away (apart from Norwich city) and I enjoyed every minute apart from the result which was a 2-0 defeat and we still hadn't scored! As we drove home from the East Midlands I could sense even my dad was becoming worried about what was coming in the coming weeks and months ahead if he was worried he never told you that but I am dead positive he was he had every right to be. The next game at the Dell, home of Southampton was vitally important in as much as we need a goal, let alone a point or two it was not to be and we lost 1-0, two points out of ten and last seasons struggle was going to repeat itself you just knew it.

School was a nightmare at the time at least I had Steedy to stick by me as the taunts came raining in and stick by me he did, he and his dad loved the Town just as myself and Dad did. Sometimes we felt just like telling them where to stick their Arsenal and Chelsea bags but it would have made no sense, they would come back twice as hard the next time, the scumbags.

The days that followed up to our next home games against Wolves and Burnley seemed again like an eternity, but playing football at school of which I had made the school team and also representing West Suffolk, helped keep my mind off it a little. The school team I played for were excellent and we had several players who were a different class none more than Johnny Haines (not the Johnny Haynes who played for Fulham & England) and Ray Hall. Johnny went on in the later years to play for Colchester United, but had to retire through serious injury and Ray Hall made the last 16 of the England Schoolboys only to be misled by several boys at school, he would have been in my eyes a top, top player in midfield for a league club somewhere in this country. Ray played in the same England schoolboys side as Ray Wilkins of Chelsea fame.

September arrived and so did Wolves, Town still looking for that first goal and it duly came courtesy of my idol Colin Viljoen, he actually scored twice but we were not to be victorious with Wolves winning 3-2, Robson really had his work cut out now to get things rolling and the visit of Burnley was to be our first win of the season. Burnley who had been a major footballing force for quite a few years were never an easy team to beat but we played well that day and goals from Baxter, Clarke and my idol Viljoen (pen) were to seal a 3-0 win and at last I could go to school with head held high albeit just for short periods. I went back to school on the Monday feeling ten foot tall that we had got a result and all we got back from the part-time fans was don't worry Col you've got Everton on Saturday, that really hit home as we were going to Goodison Park to face the champions. I never thought we would get anything and we didn't, we lost 2-0 in front of 41,000, not really a bad performance against arguably the best side in the country at the time, apart from Leeds United I suppose. We were languishing near the bottom of the table and thoughts of relegation were very much uppermost in mine and my dads mind, everybody was talking about unrest at the club, something you like to think is untrue but later in the season was to be proved totally justified, more on that later in the chapter.

But the game you always looked forward to was on the following Saturday, Manchester United at home always a huge encounter and we played it on a really hot afternoon with the pitch as always looking a picture, this was to be without doubt the best game I had seen Town play so far in my life, United came as usual with all the stars Best, Sadler, Charlton, Law the lot but Town played above themselves and never let Utd settle, goals from my idol Viljoen (2 pen), a very young and up and coming Whymark and Clarke saw off the Mancs 4-0, I just couldn't believe it. The journey home felt like two minutes and waiting to go to school seemed like two years, oh how I wanted to be at school and taunt those Manchester United followers, who only normally see one game a season and that was at Ipswich, two if Norwich were up. Although we had beaten the biggest club in the land points wise we were still not very well off and the next seven games of the season saw us pick up seven points with a draw against WBA and wins at home against Stoke, Liverpool and West Ham. The wins at home against Liverpool and West Ham were superb against teams with so many international players, things were looking up slightly. Homework from school never seemed so bad when your team had won and just at this moment all seemed not all doom and gloom, how things can change later on in the season.

Blackpool away on November 28th 1970 gave us our first away win of the season nothing too much to shout about as Blackpool were to be relegated at the end of the season, nonetheless an away win was very welcome and me and dad were starting to think maybe we can, with a little luck, rescue something from this season. We went into Christmas with only three more points added out of three games and a long winter was severely upon us, only a relegation battle and the FA Cup to look forward to and we normally go out of that in round three, but maybe this season we could have a bit of a run in the cup, you can only hope can't you. The draw was made and as usual we got not a favourable draw, away at Newcastle United at St. James' Park but the cup being the cup you always have half a chance and Town went up there and did us all proud with a 1-1 draw, goals courtesy of a very young Mick Mills no less in front of 32,000 Geordies. Now replays in those days were unlike today where they have a break for one week, we replayed three days later at Ipswich and under the lights at Ipswich we played really well against Moncur & company and won 2-1 with idol Viljoen and Hill getting the goals. It was so nice to have not only beaten a first division side, but to get into round four felt like we had won the cup and it was a brilliant feeling indeed.

The draw for round four had already been made at lunchtime, so we knew who we were playing and it was to be West Bromwich Albion away, something to look forward to because like us they were not doing particularly well in the league, so you never know, we might just might get through. Steedy and I were still taking a bit of stick at school but at least we had the cup win to chirp about and the forthcoming tie with Albion to look forward to. The next two league games up to round 4 were to be not too good as we were to lose them both and leave us in not too good a shape for the trip to the Hawthorns. I kept asking Dad if we could go to WBA, but money was a bit tight in those days and we couldn't really afford to go to a lot of away games so you just hoped and prayed and waited for the result on the telly at 4:45pm on Grandstand. Town did well again like the game at Newcastle we managed to get a draw and me and dad were ecstatic at the chance of yet another replay at Ipswich. One sad thing that came out after the game at West Brom was that Baxter had gone to the press about Robsons management and this was to prove fatal for Baxter because after several confrontations between the two and also later Tommy Carroll, the two were to be placed on the list. Baxter was duly transferred to Hull and Carroll never played much again. It was a shame about Baxter because he was a great player one of the Championship side who dad had seen right through his career and I had also been watching him for four and a half seasons and he would be a big loss but there you are you have to believe in the boss and me and dad always believed in Robson.

The replay against West Brom was eagerly awaited and just like any other night game dad was home from work like a shot. I, like always, had already had my dinner and dad after a quick wash and shave would have his and we would normally leave the house at about 05:30pm to be at Ipswich for about 06:45pm. When we got to the ground people were everywhere and because it was the cup there was extra interest you see, but this was good for the clubs finances. Nearly 26,000 were there to see Town try and get a 5th round trip away to Stoke, we were not to be disappointed as Ipswich were on top of their game and won 3-0 with Robertson, Clarke and my idol Viljoen scoring the goals. Town went off to a huge ovation at the end and it was thoroughly deserved. We were in round five and me and dad were in heaven, the first thing I asked dad in the car was if we could go to the Victoria Ground, Stoke and dad replied "We'll see son, we'll see", I could sense from his voice we might just go but you must never take anything for granted must you. Seeing Jon (Steedy) the next day at school was great, he like me was just as excited about the cup win and all the rest of the lads were pretty much struck dumb, bloody good job! When I got home from school that day I was only waiting for one thing and that was to see dad when he got home from work to see if he had made his mind upon whether we were going to Stoke, he had and said we were going, including mum! I couldn't believe it and couldn't wait for the next day to tell Steedy I was going away to watch Town in the cup, brilliant, absolutely brilliant. League form was still very much up and down but the only thing on my mind day and night was the trip to Stoke City in the FA Cup.

It was Feb 13th 1971 and we were preparing for our trip to Stoke. We were up early, very early in my case about 6am and eagerly waiting to get going. Mum had made sarnies and we had flasks of drink for the journey which we started at about 7am. After several stops on the way we arrived at Stoke at about 11am and parked on a piece of waste ground not far from the ground, again Stoke like Derby had chimneys everywhere something I was not very used to in my part of the world. Anyway we had been sitting in the car for about 15 minutes when this delightful man came out of a terraced house across the road and offered us a cup of tea on a tray, a superb gesture I thought to myself. Dad spoke to this man for a while about the game and he was absolutely convinced Stoke were going to win, suffice to say we didn't agree with him. We left the car and went to the ground, found where we were sitting, yes sitting believe it or not and a great view it was too, I couldn't believe how big the ground looked as I was only used to 30,000 at our place, 36,000 were in and there was still room for more. Town defended for their lives that day and at 0-0 at half time we were well happy and all I wanted at the time was the final whistle. Second half was mostly one way traffic for Stoke but we managed to hang on and draw 0-0 a fantastic result and I couldn't wait for next week and the replay at Ipswich. As soon as we got in the car to travel home we put the radio on to see how the great Leeds United side had got on at Colchester United, I could not believe it they had lost 3-2 with legend Crawford getting two, that result certainly made the journey home not too bad at all.

The replay on the following Tuesday was the really big game of the season and Portman Road was packed, absolutely packed with gates locked half an hour before kick off with 30,000 inside. We all went to the game that night apart from Mum and I thought we had a really good chance of making the last eight, Town played alright on the night but were beaten by the only goal of the game, a Dennis Smith header up the North Stand end, a killer blow for everyone. I remember everybody coming out of the ground very disheartened including me, I don't think I said a word all the way home, I was gutted. All was left was to make sure we stayed in the first division, two games against Arsenal and Leeds were to follow and no points to show, although we put up an almighty performance against Leeds at home losing 4-2 with goals from Hill and Viljoen, never a disgrace to lose to Arsenal (eventual Champions) or Leeds United. Two wins followed against Manchester City (Viljoen, Clarke) and Newcastle United when flying winger Robertson notched so things were not all bad although we still had an awful lot to do. The next seven games were to be disastrous as regards results and we only picked up three points out of fourteen and the comedians at school had started again, out of the cup and staring relegation in the face, what do you expect? The only person in the world to keep me sane was my dad who always said they wouldn't go down, I always believed him but sometimes just wondered will they? The next five or six weeks were to prove very important but three points out of fourteen was not very inspiring and it was going to go to the wire that was for sure and so it did.

Our next win was to be against WBA away a superb win at the Hawthorns to give us a little breathing space, with Burnley and Blackpool almost doomed, Town were looking like First Division football would be there again next season and sure enough with a win over Huddersfield Town at home (Hill and Clarke) it was safe. Three games left Man Utd away (2-3), Wolves away (0-0) followed by our last home game against Chelsea where we drew 0-0 and Robson had kept us in the First Division again with something to build on, one hopes, leading scorer was Viljoen my idol again with 12 goals from midfield a fine effort indeed. I could enjoy my summer holidays again and look forward to next season with the hope it would not be so much of a struggle as it had been in the last two years.

8 - ROBSON MAKES HIS MARK - 1971-1972

Although still firmly a Town fan, apart from the odd occasion when he would look for West Ham's result, it really was from now on that me and my dad would be as one as far as supporting Town was concerned. John had other interests in life at this time notably the ATC (Air Training Corp) and later on had a big love of motorbikes of which he would ride his BSA for hours upon end with his mate Steve Westley, also a firm Town fan. The close season had seen a big change at my beloved Portman Road as the old East Stand (the Chicken Run) had been knocked down and replaced with a fine new structure on the East side with seats at the top and terrace at the bottom it really was a fine new stand and was remarkably constructed within 102 days and available for use by the time Everton were to visit on the opening day of the season in August.

The season was to start with a 0-0 draw with Everton, not a bad result considering the scousers were champions only two season ago and had a host of international players. We went home after the first game full of belief that Town could do a whole lot better this season especially after the signing of Bryan Hamilton from Linfield who had a fine close home international series and also a fine debut in Towns midfield. Myself and Steedy would talk about Town all the time at school during our breaks and after the Everton game we were convinced it would not be another season of struggle. This season we were to play our first two games at home and the next team to come to Portman Road were Coventry City on the following Tuesday night something I always loved, night games and Town were not to let us down winning 3-1 with goals from Clarke (2) and Hamilton, whose first goal it was for the club. So we had secured three points from a possible four at the start of the season and things looked very promising but the next five games, Southampton and West Ham away both 0-0 draws, Leeds at home, a 0-2 loss, Derby at home 0-0 and Man Utd away 0-1 saw us not score a goal but at least we had secured some vital points to build our season, dad was convinced we had a better side, and who was I to argue with him he had after all seen us win the title, something I could only dream about.

With one Irishman on board in Bryan Hamilton, Robson decided another was to come in and what a signing he proved to be, it was Allan Hunter from Blackburn Rovers a centre half who to be honest I didn't know too much about. But boy was he to make an impact in future seasons, he was to become a colossus and a very firm favourite with the fans. He made his debut in a 2-1 home defeat to Leicester, four days after we had lost at home to Man Utd 3-1 in the League Cup a night which would always live long in my memory when a certain section of the crowd were calling for Robsons head, an absolute disgrace in my mind and I still to this day hope those so called fans are eating their words. Robson fortunately got the backing of the board which pleased my dad as he always was a big fan of the passionate Geordie. Robson came back strong from all of this and we went to one of our favourite hunting grounds and came back with a 2-1 win at West Brom with Robson's double signings of 1969-1970 scoring the goals, Robertson and Clarke.

My own football career at schoolboy level was still going very well and I was selected to play for the full Suffolk side this season which really did make my dad proud and I was later in the season to play at Luton Towns ground a very proud moment for myself because I had never before played on a league ground. Mixing schoolboy football and watching Town was proving very difficult but I managed it somehow because my love for the Town was always so much I had to be there. The next five games were to secure us five points with three draws and a win against Stoke City at home with a brace from Mick Hill. At this time Mr Robson decided we needed some more strength up front and he went out and signed Rod Belfitt from Leeds Utd who struggled to get in the Leeds team at the time with the likes of Clarke, Jones etc, I had seen him on Match of the Day several times and he was to prove a decent signing for us.

Rod Belfitts debut was to be in our home game in November against Wolves linking up with Mick Hill, nearly 22,000 were there to witness a 2-1 win and a winning start for Belfitt, the crowd took to him because he was an honest sort of a player and also a pretty good finisher. Robson was bit by bit starting to assemble a team that maybe just maybe would be able to hold their own more comfortably in the top flight. After another two games of which we drew 1-1 at Palace with Belfitt scoring again and a 1-0 win at home to Huddersfield (Hill) came what was to become one of the biggest embarrassments of my football watching years. It was November 27th 1971 and we were away to Sheff Utd a day I will never forget in my lifetime, we were doing okay in the league but no one could have predicted the outcome on that day in Yorkshire, the result 0-7 and Woodward scored four times, I remember listening to the result on Grandstand with dad in total disbelief. The first thing what came to mind was school on Monday and boy did I take a hammering, but never mind, I took it on the chin because now was the time when I said to myself don't worry, there's always next weekend because we had got to the time when losing every week just wasn't an option. Our next two home games were Liverpool (0-0) and Man Utd (0-0) both draws and no goals but two very good points against very good opposition considering we had not long taken an almighty bashing at Bramall Lane.

Christmas was with us again and me and John had got our usual presents, games, socks etc. and also our usual stocking with oranges, playing cards inside it you know we all get them don't we. After the Christmas dinner had been consumed along with tea later all my thoughts would be on the Christmas game and this season it was Chelsea away on the 27th December. Now Chelsea away never gave me and my dad any confidence because it was our bogey ground we never won there and this season was to be no different as we lost 2-0 in front of 43,000 very loud cockneys. We were going through a little sticky patch in our season but dad kept saying we would come through it, WBA home lost (2-3) and a 2-2 draw at Leeds where Hunter scored his first goal for Town were not bad results but a win against WBA would have put us in slightly better spirits going into the FA Cup. The FA cup draw saw us paired with Peterborough United and it was to be the first time I was to go away to a game by myself. Some older friends of mine in Bury St. Edmunds had arranged a coach trip to Peterborough and what a trip it turned out to be.

We met up at about 9am and arrived at London Road at about 11 o'clock after a couple of stops on the way, probably something to do with the lads at the back wanting to go to the toilet, singing on the bus was loud and it wasn't to get any quieter in the ground believe me. As soon as we got off the bus the older lad's that I knew were making a beeline for the pub, I went with them but only had a coke, honest! After leaving the pub at about 1:15pm we made for the ground and I couldn't wait to get in to see my first away game on my own. Town came out wearing a yellow and blue away strip I really liked and still think was one of their best. Quite a decent crowd was there, about 17,000, of which at least 4,000 were Town fan's singing away. The game could have been a banana skin but Town played well and my idol Viljoen and lanky Mick Hill scored the goals in a 2-0 win, the fourth round had been reached and the journey home like any other away game, never seems so long when you have won. It was strange going to a game away without my dad but it was good, if not a bit intimidating and I'm sure he worried about me all afternoon but I got home safe and that's all that mattered. Back to school on Monday and me and Steedy just weren't getting the stick we used to thank's to Robson finally getting a team to be proud of. I ran home from school at dinner time to hear the draw and we drew Birmingham away, a second division side going well, but the tie was winnable or so we thought!

Two league games went by before the tie, a 1-1 draw at Coventry and a 1-0 win at home to West Ham thanks to "diesel" Morris a result I always enjoyed because me and dad loved it when we beat London clubs it was always a bit special. I had craved dad since we beat Peterborough if we could go to St Andrews and he gave in, we were going. Just for a change dad said "shall we go on the Blue Arrow?" that was a train put on for some games just for Town fans, so go on the train we did, it was just me and dad as mum and

John didn't very often come anymore, the journey didn't seem too bad and we were there at Birmingham station at about 1pm. Apart from the odd trip to London this was obviously the biggest place I had ever seen, we walked from the station to the ground (about 20 minutes) and when we got there I was stunned, the place seemed so big compared to dear old Portman Road.

We stood on a terrace on the side with some Ipswich fans but we were surrounded by brummies 41,000 of them it was a bit scary and I remember them singing keep right on to the end of the road, you must have been able to hear them at the Hawthorns. The game itself was fairly even but Birmingham won it with the only goal, for a 1-0 win, by the way that was the first time I had seen a very young Trevor Francis play and what a player he was. So we trudged back to the station having been knocked out of the cup again, I really did start wondering if we would ever do anything in the cup, there's always next year I suppose. Anyway, I suppose it was maybe a good thing because staying in Division One was obviously the main objective and was definitely always the main priority of Robson and Cyril Lea. The next nine league games would see us not really performing as we should and only 5 points were to be picked up, we surely needed a very good finish and it duly started with a fine home win against Spurs with a Want own goal and another goal by Rod Belfitt. The next two games were away to Newcastle where we won 1-0 thanks to young Trevor Whymark, who was just starting to become a regular and a 3-1 win at relegation side Huddersfield with Belfitt, Morris and Robertson on the scoresheet. Next up and a game I was very much looking forward to was at home to Sheff Utd, that team that had put seven past us earlier in the season, would we get revenge? No, but at least we didn't concede in a 0-0 draw.

Town had finished the season very well indeed and myself and dad were very much looking forward to the visit of a very good Man City side, Doyle, Bell, Summerbee & Co, they had had a very good season eventually finishing fourth, but we were more than their equal on the day and we turned them over 2-0 with Whymark and Harper scoring the goals. Safety was guaranteed for another season and we finished off with a trip to Anfield, not good because we never win there and this season was to be no different as we lost 2-0 in front of 54,316 scousers, some things never change. All in all it had been a good season with Ipswich finishing 13th in the league, and only losing 15 games out of 42 a very good effort and Robson had really began to make his mark at Portman Road.

9 - TOWN BECOME A FORCE
1972-1973

During the summer and having just left school I decided to write to Ipswich Town for a trial as I had just had quite a successful season with West Suffolk and Suffolk at schoolboy level. I knew about the youth policy at Town and after talking to my dad decided to give it a go, I received a letter back about two weeks later with Towns crest on the front of the envelope, I couldn't believe it, I had got a trial at the club I loved so much. It was on a Sunday and dad drove me over to Portman Road along with my mate from down the road Steve Lockwood. When I got there I was very nervous and dad being dad said "don't worry son, you'll be okay" but I was still very nervous as I walked into the hallowed dressing rooms at Portman Road. The trialists of whom had come from all over the British Isles were very nice lads and I remember talking to one lad who had come all the way down from Scotland that was what I was up against!

We changed in the away dressing room and wore the Ipswich away strip of yellow and blue, I made a beeline for the number 8 and duly got it, there I was having my trial for Town and wearing my idols number 8, just for a moment I thought I was Colin Viljoen. The trial started and we were playing against Towns youth of which they included several lads who later that season would go on and win the FA Youth Cup, they were exceptional players and out of all the trialist only two played the whole 90 minutes, suffice to say I was not one of them, I had a poor game and was taken off after 70 minutes and didn't go back on, I was heartbroken.

On the way home dad tried to cheer me up by saying well you'll just have to try again somewhere, but I never did and looking back now I wish I had. Back in the 70's it was a time that if you hadn't had a grammar school background you just got on with it and found a job or apprenticeship, I decided along with quite a few of my mates to get a job to earn some money. So I got a job down Watsons Builders Yard picking orders. It was okay at the time and gave me a bit of money to fund my obsession of watching Town play. After all the events of the summer and me finding myself a job the season kicked off with Town going to play Man Utd at Old Trafford, now I could think of easier places to go than there, but Town were to set their stall out for the season with a 2-1 win with Whymark and Hamilton scoring in front of 51,000. That day also saw the start of a career of an absolute legend, it was the debut of a very young Kevin Beattie who marked George Best out of the game and became an instant hit with the Town fans. After gaining what was two superb points on the opening day of the season, our next game was against promoted Norwich City and we were really up for it, on a balmy Tuesday night in August.

Dad had left off early for the local derby and had just enough time for a sandwich before we set off at about 5:15pm for the ground. There were fans everywhere when we got there and the Norwich fans were put into the Churchmans end of the ground. 30,000 had turned up to see Norwich spoil the party and win 2-1, Bryan Hamilton getting Towns only goal of the night. It was an unbelievable result for me and dad and we trekked off to the car thinking well at least it's only the second game of the season, how right we were proved to be. After such a shock defeat to that lot down the round, the next seven games in the league were to put us right up there with the best, Birmingham at home (2-0), Leeds away (3-3), Newcastle away (2-1), Sheff Utd away (0-0), Spurs home (1-1), Southampton away (2-1) and Stoke home (2-0) was to shape our season and really make people stand up and stare. Work was really enjoyable at the time with several Town fans down there, and we also had a few Man Utd fans, it was so good taking the mick out of them when we were doing well.

The league cup came and went as was normal, it was a competition I really don't know why we bothered to enter, we never did well and this season was no exception as after beating lowly Newport 3-0, we lost at home to Stoke 2-1 and Wembley was just a dream again as usual. At this time of my fanatical footballing life I used to talk to dad all the time about formations, winning leagues, cups, anything and he would love it as much as me, he couldn't wait for the next game to come. Town were to have a blip with their next four games, Chelsea away (0-2), Leicester home (0-2), West Ham home (1-1) and Arsenal away (0-1) was to see us drop a bit and after beating Derby 3-1 and drawing at Everton 2-2 Robson was to shock all the Town fans by buying an unknown David Johnson from Everton with Belfit going the other way, it was to prove a master stroke from Bobby Robson in future months ahead. Leeds Utd were next up at home for Johnsons debut and Town came away with a fine 2-2 draw with goals from Madeley (og) and Whmark who was really making his mark up front this season with firstly Belfitt and now Johnson.

The following game was the derby game at Norwich and for the first time I went not with dad but with my mate Kev on the train, it was great fun going on the train packed full of Town fans and not a Norwich fan to be seen. Those were the days when fan's had scarves around their wrists, trousers or jeans above their air ware boots. Yes it was the skinhead era and I was no exception as was Kev. The train rolled into Norwich station about 11:30am, time to go and have a couple of pints and a good old sing-song pre-match before we with about 5,000 others walked down along the river to Carrow Road. The atmosphere away in a derby was always so much more special and this one was no different, the game was so fast and furious and ended 0-0, probably just as well it always helped the police if it was a draw.

The season was going really well and the next nine league games were to bring 14 points, a brilliant haul of points and Town were right up there fighting for a place in Europe. Both myself and dad could hardly believe it, but it was happening right in front of our eyes. FA Cup time was with us again and Town were to be drawn away at Chelmsford City, a non league side from Essex, what a draw I just had to go, and go I did. Although still going to home games with dad I had started to go to quite a few away games with lots of my different friends. I had got my ticket from Ipswich for the tie and booked a ticket on the train to go to Chelmsford, this was to be a great day out with us arriving at about 11am and heading for the first watering hole we could find, after a few jars we had to walk across this big park to the ground (New Writtle Street). About 4,500 Town fans were there, and because it was non-league against First Division. Match of the Week were there to televise it, just in case. It was typically non-league inside with little snack bars and the like, but Ipswich were totally professional about the game and won 3-1 with goals from Harper, Johnson and Hamilton, it was a great relief to me because if we had lost you would never hear the end of it. Travelling home on the train was fun singing and dancing and wondering who we would get in round four, we were soon to find out it was to be Chelsea away, great just what we wanted, I don't think, we never win at Chelsea.

The talk in the pubs about Town was very much changing, a few seasons ago they were always the joke if you like, but now people were really starting to take them seriously. It was very good on the ear I can tell you. Spurs away were next up and Town went down there and beat them 1-0 with the goal from Hamilton who was becoming a goal-scoring expert from midfield, next were Southampton at home and my idol Viljoen (pen) and Hamilton again scored in a 2-2 draw which very much kept us in the thick of things at the top of the league. Cup week was upon us and me and dad had decided not to go to Chelsea as it was our bogey ground. I'm glad we didn't as yes, you've guessed it we lost 2-0 in front of 36,000. I just knew it would happen, I don't know why we bother to travel to the bridge we always got beat, another Wembley dream over. Although out of the cup the club was going from strength to strength and together with our good league form we were also going well in the Texaco Cup, having beaten St. Johnstone from Scotland, Wolves and Newcastle so a final against Norwich in May to look forward to. Man Utd were next in town in the league and it was a day before my birthday, what a present it would be to turn them over, I always felt confident as anything when we played them, it was as if we were playing Colchester United. The game went the same way as it normally does with Town out playing them to win 4-1 with Hamilton (2), Harper and Viljoen (pen) netting the goals. After this superb win the run to the end of the season was to be very disappointing as we only collected ten points from the last 13 games but it was still enough to clinch a place in the UEFA

Cup and cement our position in fourth in the league. The Texaco Cup final against Norwich was played over two legs, 2-1 at home, 2-1 away (4-2 on agg) and to make it a double for the club the youths went on to win the FA Youth Cup for the first time in the clubs history, a fine achievement.

10 - FIRST TASTE OF EUROPE
1973-1974

Winning the Texaco Cup albeit not the FA Cup and also lifting the FA Youth Cup had got me thinking that Town at last had become a club to be reckoned with. Also qualifying for the UEFA Cup was a dream come true and me and dad couldn't wait for the draw. When it was made and we found out we had drawn Real Madrid it was a game we were all looking forward to more than any other.

Our season started with more or less the squad we had finished with the previous season and the more players like the legend Beattie played the better they got. Robson was a manager who based his whole philosophy on astute signing and the development of youth and he was king at both, more youth were to be brought in as the season developed, Burley, Talbot to name but two. Robson was to sell David Best later in the season and Laurie Sivell at 5"4 was to play a decent part of the season at the end.

Ipswich kicked off the season with a home game against Leicester a team we were always capable of beating so me and dad were quite disappointed when we only got a 1-1 draw, but at least we hadn't been beaten, I hated it when you lost the first game it puts you straight on to the back foot in the season. Whymark and Johnson had really started to hit it off up front and they were to share the goals in the next game away at West Ham with the result being 3-3, Johnson getting 2 and Trev the other. Two games later with a 3-0 defeat at Everton and a 3-1 home defeat at Newcastle got us thinking what has gone on here, only two points from four games but we always had faith in Robson to turn it round and turn it round he did. Man Utd were next up and I remember always saying to Dad "don't worry we'll get the points today we're only playing Utd, we always beat them". It was always such a good atmosphere when you played Utd, they always brought a lot of fans and the singing was loud, very loud. The game was fast and furious and goals by Johnson and Lambert sealed a 2-1 win, another two points off Utd, oh how they hated playing at Portman Road.

The season had not got off to a brilliant start and was to further go downhill with the next two games in the league, dad kept saying they would pick up, but I wished they would start soon, as after a 3-1 defeat at Newcastle and a 1-1 draw at Stoke things were not looking rosy, going into one of the biggest games in the clubs history at home to Real Madrid in the UEFA cup. Now work was going ok, but like school before, when you had a game like Madrid coming up everything seems to take forever, the days seemed like weeks, but eventually September 19th 1973 came along and the realisation of the fact we were going to see one of the greatest club sides ever in the world at our ground, brilliant. The crowd wasn't as big as I had expected on the night, just above 25,000 but when the two teams came out side by side with Mills holding the pennant in his hand you just knew that yes, we are there with the big boys. The game was typically European with Madrid just holding out for a draw, but in the second half Portman Road exploded when Rubian put through his own goal up the North Stand end. I couldn't believe it. We were 1-0 up against the great Real Madrid and hold out we did for the rest of the game to record a famous victory. All me and dad talked about going home was if, and it was a big if, we could hold them in Madrid, we were to see on the 3rd October 1973. Miracles sometimes happen, don't they. The result against Madrid was to inspire Ipswich tremendously and the next two league games were both won with a 3-2 win against Burnley and a 3-0 win at St. Andrews four very vital points going into the game in Madrid. Radio commentary had only just started on local radio and it was great to hear the game live, but I have to admit it was one of the longest 90 minutes of my life. 80,000 were packed into the Bernabeu Stadium baying for Ipswichs blood, but my oh how they defended and Best was exceptional in a fantastic 0-0 draw. Ipswich had done it, they had turned over Real Madrid over two legs absolutely phenomenal.

Games were coming thick and fast but really all me and my dad wanted to see was us do well in the league and sure enough because of the result in Spain, results really picked up. We were going well in the league with only one defeat in the next eight games and that was to Liverpool away, where we never won, 12 points were picked up in that time, taking us again well up the table towards the top.

In between those league games we were to draw Lazio in the UEFA Cup, another big name in Europe with a reputation for dirty football, they were not to let anyone down, indeed, in fact I thought they were worse than people had made out. Town were at home first again, and we went for the throat straight away, playing all the football while Lazio only wanted to waste time and kick anything that moved. But they were to get the biggest shock of their lives because they just could not live with us and a brace in both halves from Whymark gave us a 4-0 win, a superb performance against a disgraceful side, and an excellent four goals by Whymark. The return game in Italy was even more disgraceful as for as Lazio were concerned, again we were all huddled up at home listening to the game on the Radio, and with Lazio 2-0 up at half time we were starting to fear the worst, but second half goals from my idol Viljoen (pen) and Johnson meant we were eventually to lose 4-2 on the night and go through 6-4 on aggregate. Events after the final whistle were awful as far as the players and Town fans were concerned as bottles and other objects were thrown at both players and fans, defeat was just what the doctor ordered for them. The UEFA cup had firmly took hold of me and my dad and we could not wait for the next draw to be made, it was to be FC Twente from Holland, a nice change from what we had been watching from those yobs of Italy.

It was late November when Twente came over here for the 1st leg and they played some very good football as all Dutch teams in the 70s did, but didn't have enough to stop Town gaining the advantage with a 1-0 win, again Whymark who was becoming a top European goal scorer getting the goal. I must admit I was not totally convinced the one nill would be enough going to Holland, but having seen what we had done before in Europe it gave me and dad a bit of hope. The second leg as with all games before we got round the radio and listened to the whole game, oh how I wished I was to be there away in Europe but that was to come later when I was a bit older. Town played really well but always did against footballing sides and won on the night 2-1 with goals from Morris and Hamilton to go through 3-1 on aggregate. Here I was in my first season watching European football and we were in round four, it was quite amazing really. We had a long wait for the next round because in those days you went from early December to early March before the last eight started, a good thing because everybody could concentrate again on league and FA Cup.

The next two league games against Leeds at home and Southampton away were lost followed by a good win at home to Birmingham 3-0 and that brought us to the boxing day clash at Norwich. Again we all went on the train as was the norm in those days for the trip to Norwich, thousands of Town fans were there to see Town play Norwich who were struggling big time in the league. A Johnson penalty and Lambert scored the goals for a 2-1 derby win and that set up your perfect Christmas, forget the presents it was just so nice to beat the old enemy again on their patch. The Barclay end packed with Norwich fans were very quiet while the North Stand lads who had made the journey were ecstatic, especially on the way back to the station when the ribbing really started.

The FA Cup was only just round the corner and I said to dad perhaps this season as we were playing so well might be our season, a draw at home to Sheff Utd was promising and in a superb end to end cup tie we edged it 3-2 with the Beat (Kevin Beattie) getting two and Hamilton getting the other, I sensed walking back to the car after we might just do something this season and I think so did dad. On Monday lunch time we had drawn Man Utd away, not bad, although it was away because Utd had been struggling big time in the league all season. With one win, one defeat and a draw going into the cup game at Old Trafford, we went up there with a lot of confidence and sure enough the lads came back with a 1-0 win thanks to a goal from Kevin Beattie, we were in round five and for once thought we had half-a-chance, that was until the draw on Monday, when we got Liverpool away. Ipswich started being talked about more and more on TV and Radio and we were actually being shown more and more on Match of the Day, which was a nice change from Leeds, Arsenal, Liverpool and Man Utd, but there you go who wants to show a team near the bottom eh Utd!

Next up at Portman Road is a game that will always live with me, it was Southampton at home on a Saturday evening and that night was really the very first time somebody got a real hiding, it was always going to come. Town were superb on the night and Saints could not live with them as we rattled up seven goals on the night to win 7-0, the poor old Saints keeper didn't know what had hit him. Two league games followed with a defeat to West Ham and a win at Turf Moor against Burnley 1-0 before we went to Anfield for that FA Cup tie. Now as I have said before at the time we never won at Anfield and this game would be no exception as we went out 2-0 a result that didn't surprise me at all, the Wembley dream over against, always next season eh. We were to draw the next three league games against Spurs, Chelsea and Norwich before we re-embarked on the European scene with a quarter final against Lokomotive Leipzig. There was a great atmosphere in the ground for the first leg and without a whole lot of luck combined with some good goalkeeping Leipzig would have been dead and buried. But we were not to be denied on the night because we won the tie with a second half goal from Beattie, a slender lead but we had done it before and we would have to see if we could do it again. The second leg in two weeks time was a game no Town fan including me will forget, leading just one nil from the first leg, we started not too bad and were still in front on aggregate at the break, but in the second half we conceded the all important goal for Leipzig and it's 1-1 on the night and on aggregate. Full time arrived so we went into extra time, still there is no further scoring and for the first time in our history we went to penalties, the boys couldn't quite make it and we lost 4-3 on spot kicks, a real body blow to everybody connected with the club including me, I was devastated, bloody devastated. After being consoled at home by my dad it was to be to dream of what might have been, but when all the dust had settled and I came to realise what a great effort the boys had made and gave myself and my dad some very happy memories.

Back to work and also down the pub to receive the stick that all football fans get, but not to worry because they knew deep down that Town had really arrived at the top level. After defeat in Leipzig it was back to the every day battle in the league and hopeful qualify again for a competition we had done so well in, me and dad went up again to Derby County for our next game, we lost 2-0 but no one was going to have a go at the team after such a demanding fixture list. We needed to get back on track and we sure did with four wins and a draw coming from the last seven games, Europe had been reached again and Norwich finished bottom, perfect just perfect. At the end of the season, Peter Morris was sold to Norwich and Paul Cooper brought in from Birmingham, Cooper was to wait quite a long time for his chance in goal as the position went to Laurie Sivell.

Real Madrid Pennant

11 - CLOSE OH SO CLOSE 1974-1975

At seventeen years old, and just having had my first holiday away with my mates down Cornwall, which was quite an experience, it was back to work and wanting for yet another season of pure heaven. I had changed my job and was now working for S.M engineering a firm up Northern Way in Bury St Edmunds as a storeman, the pay was better than what I had been getting before and because of that I was able to fund my obsessions a little easier from now on. Manchester United and Norwich had been relegated the previous season, which although was very nice, I said to myself during the close season, we won't be able to take eight points off them, shame, but there you go that's life.

We started the season against the north London giants Arsenal and Spurs away, not an easy start by any stretch of the imagination, but the results of both which were both 1-0 wins was to put us right on track for quite a memorable season. Myself and dad had by this time gone our separate ways at the game, I still went with him in the car, but when I got to the ground more often than not I stood with my mates in the North stand, this was to be the way of it for three or four years until I got married apart from away games of course. Burnley were first up at Ipswich and with our points already in the bag optimism was very high at the ground and we were not disappointed as goals from Talbot and Whymark kept the winning run going, six points out of six, what a start. Mick Lambert had become quite a regular feature in the team by now and it was in front of nearly 28,000 that he scored twice and Beattie got the other in a 3-0 win against Arsenal, twice beaten in seven days, absolutely brilliant. After the game with Arsenal, like most London clubs in the 70s and early 80s, you kept your head down, because like most big clubs in the 70s they had a big following of absolute idiots, the skinhead era. It was very frightening on occasions seeing people chased after and beaten up, cars wrecked and shops smashed up, but it was with us, and you dealt with it the best you could, nobody was going to stop my obsession, no one. Apart from a defeat at Sheff United, Town were to win eight of their first nine games, a run which took us to the top of the table, champions possibly? Our main rivals that season were again to be Derby County and Liverpool. Derby who had won the title in 71-72 were a formidable outfit with the likes of Todd, McFarland, Nish & Co, they really were a very good side.

The UEFA cup which the previous season had gone so well was to be very disappointing, a home game in the first leg against FC Twente was drawn 2-2, not a very good result in Europe considering the away goals they scored. It was to prove decisive as we went to Holland and drew 1-1, out of the competition on away goals an absolute sickner, but it was to help us in later months with the build up of fixtures in the cup which was to come. Four defeats in the league in the next five games in September and October saw us drop a bit in the league but Robson always maintained we would get it back on track and he was always generally right. The football we had been treated to over the last three or four seasons was a joy to watch and this season was proving just the same thanks to Mr Robson. We stopped the rot with a 1-1 draw at home to Man City and the next game at home to Liverpool was a cracker as all our games with the scousers were.

Over 30,000 were in the ground for the big one, a game which could have a big bearing on where the title lands up. I was as usual in my place in the North Stand and got pushed about 20 steps down the terrace as Talbot scored to give us a 1-0 win, a big step in the right direction towards the title. It was always my ambition as a supporter to see Town, who had become a big force in English football, win the league, it came I suppose from a tiny piece of jealousy of knowing my dad had seen them win it in the 60s. Dad was good to me though, and I know for an absolute fact he was willing them to win the title just for me, he was like that, an absolute diamond of a man. The next nine league games taking us to Christmas were either won or lost, we never drew one game at all, we won five and lost four of which one of the defeats was against Derby away who were eventually to go and win the title. Another one of the defeats which I still believe cost us the title was on Boxing day we were at home to Luton Town, a poor side that season and we were all over them, it was just one of those days when nothing would go in and we got caught on the break for one of their only attacks, I couldn't believe it, it totally messed my Christmas up altogether. The season up till Christmas had been a superb effort and the emergence of more quality youth teamers was coming through all the time with George Burley this season being the prime example, a seventeen year old who had adapted to the first division so well.

Once again the FA Cup was upon us and when we were drawn out to play Wolves away at Molineux who was to know what was in store for us all in that cup season. We went to Wolves very confident we could get a result and sure enough a Viljoen free kick and a Johnson header saw us through. The next round saw us paired with Liverpool, a brilliant tie for everyone, both teams were in the top three of the league and going well, 34,709 in the ground for of which at least 6,000 must have been scousers. A superb game looked to be heading for a replay at Anfield when believe it or not a certain Mick Mills arrived in the area in the 90th minute to stab home past Clemence, dreamland, absolute dreamland, we were through against the mighty Liverpool. We won three games out of the next four in the league to keep us right up there, but on Feb 8th, Liverpool were to get their revenge for the cup defeat when they beat us 5-2 at Anfield, in a real thriller which was on Match of the Day. Beattie and Whymark scoring for Town.

Town though had other things on their mind the next Saturday as me and dad prepared ourselves for the 5th round of the cup at home to Aston Villa. Again another big crowd of over 31,000 came to cheer Town on and into the quarter finals, it was to become an epic encounter as Villa really came at Town and were leading the game until a masterstroke from Robson changed everything. With time running out and Town 2-1 down, Robson brought on Hamilton as sub, and what a substitution it turned out to be as Hamilton scored twice and we went on to win 3-2, the crowd were going wild and I was just on top of the world dreaming of who we would get in the draw on Monday. I listened to the draw on the radio at work on the Monday and we were drawn to play Leeds Utd at home, a good draw against the mighty Leeds who my best friend Kev supported. Down the pub for the next few days it was all talk about the tie and who would get through, I don't think Kev was totally over the moon with the prospect, although it was a nice shorter journey for him, rather than the 180 miles he used to have to do in his VW to see a game.

A defeat at Coventry (1-3) and a superb home win against eventual champions Derby (3-0) set us up nicely for the game against Leeds. Tickets for the game had been selling well and eventually 38,010 were at the game which was a club record and still is. Leeds had brought about 8,000 with them, not a nice thought considering their awful reputation for crowd violence, but on the day they were not too bad thank god. Me and dad stood together that day in the Churchmans stand praying for a good result. Leeds were strong in those days and we would have to play exceptionally well to beat them. The game was something of a stalemate with both sides cancelling each other out and it duly ended 0-0 with a replay at Elland Road. Going home I asked dad if we were going to go to the replay, he replied "have a word with Kev, see what he's doing", so I did and arranged to go to Leeds with my Friend Kevin in his car.

For the replay we left Bury at about 3pm, arriving in Leeds at about 6:45pm, Leeds fans everywhere, 50,000 of 'em not a nice sight I can assure you. Kev was standing in the Kop at Leeds that night and we asked him before the game which stand we should stand in, he suggested the side stand, which although full of Leeds fans wasn't too bad. We went 1-0 up through a goal from David Johnson, not a good idea at Leeds, but we kept fairly quiet and just hoped we could hang on, we did until about 5 minutes before time and Leeds equalised. I remember saying to dad during the break we would never hang on in extra time we did thanks mainly to Kevin Beattie who was outstanding all night. The journey home felt a long one as it was very late at night and we had had quite an exhausting evening, but all told everybody was fairly happy at the 1-1 draw and we now had to wait for the next replay which was to be at Leicester Citys ground.

The league season was still going very well and with two wins out of three against Newcastle (5-4) and also 2-1 away win at Stoke we went into the third game with Leeds bang in form. For the second replay I travelled up with Dad in his car and we arrived in Leicester at about 5:30pm, enough time to walk up the city and have a bit to eat and a drink. Filbert Street was packed to the rafters that night with about 18,000 fans from both sides there to witness another 0-0 draw after extra time. Both sides gave their all but the defences again were on top form along with some great goalkeeping, so there we were going home thinking about when the next replay was to be, it was to be two days later on the Thursday at the same ground, would I go of course I will. Dad couldn't get the time off work so quickly for the third replay, so I decided to go with Kev in his VW. There was nowhere near as many at the fourth game, mainly because of how near it was to the last game and also because I suppose people were running out of money. The game itself was to prove to be a classic with Town always the more likely to come out on top, the game finished 3-2 to Ipswich with Clive Woods getting the winner with a superb curling effort in the top corner, a fine way to end what had been a cup marathon with Leeds United, Wembley this year? Who knows!

The draw for the semi final had been made quite a while ago and we were to be paired with West Ham at Villa Park, a game we really thought we were more than capable of winning. We had three league games before we played West Ham to keep us in with a chance to win the league and Leicester (2-1), Chelsea away (0-0) and a home win against Birmingham (3-2) kept us right in the picture as we embarked on our first ever FA Cup Semi Final. Me and dad booked on the coach for the Semi Final and we left the Angel Hill at about 9am bound for Sunny Birmingham. We arrived at the services at about midday, parking in the coach park at Villa alongside hundreds of other Town coaches, 29,000 Town fans had brought tickets for the game and me and dad were standing in the Holte end of the ground. West Ham were not a bad side at the time, with Bonds etc. but it certainly was a game we were very much expected to win and me and dad were absolutely convinced we would be at Wembley come 4:45. The atmosphere at Villa Park was immense with the Town fans at the Holte end making a wall of sound as the boys came out. Ipswich were wearing their change strip of yellow and blue on the day, a strip I always very much liked, the game was very much in West Ham's half most of the time but we just could not get that vital breakthrough. West Ham defended for the most part of the game with the occasional attack but never really threatened, the game was marred in the second half when Beattie broke his arm and would miss the replay at Stamford Bridge, the game ending 0-0. The journey home on the coach was high spirited as well as we all thought it was just a matter of time before we got what we deserved.

The replay which was played at Chelsea, something of an unfair advantage we thought beings we were playing West Ham, was played four days later under the lights. Again me and dad went on the coach and arrived in London at around 6:30pm. There were West Ham fans everywhere as a lot of tickets were actually being sold on the night at the ground. Once inside the Bridge it was quite obvious we were outnumbered as regards support about 25,000 of the 45,000 crowd being West Ham fans. This didn't really bother me and dad because we still thought we had the class to win though, how wrong we would be proved to be. West Ham played better than in the first game at Villa, but I suppose anyone can do a whole lot better when you are playing with 12 men. The reason I say that is because of Clive Thomas, who still to this day I believe cheated us, yes CHEATED US. We scored two perfectly good goals on the night, only to see them both ruled out, something Thomas wrote about later when he retired and in hindsight said they both should have stood, thanks Clive, I don't think. The game actually finished 2-1 to West Ham with both goals from Taylor who was to go on against Fulham in the final and score two more in a 2-0 win to win the cup, no consolations for us though. When we did eventually get on the bus home, I can quite openly admit I cried. I couldn't believe we had lost to West Ham. It was so disappointing to get so close, oh so close. I went to work the next day and hardly spoke to anyone, it just was as if someone had died, that's how I felt and it lasted for days.

We got it all out of our systems the following Saturday when we played QPR at home and beat them 2-1 with goals by Hamilton and Whymark, the last three games were to see us lose 2-1 at Leeds, draw 1-1 at Maine Road and on the last day we got total revenge as we stuffed the cockneys 4-1. West Ham arrived on the last day all cocky before their cup final but Town were out to maul them and maul them we did. Town were brilliant on the day and goals from Talbot, Whymark, Beattie and Big Al (Hunter) wrapped up another brilliant season which saw us finish third in the table, only 2pts behind Derby and reach our first cup semi final, Europe bound again. The season was totally capped off when the Youths won the FA Youth Cup for the second time in three seasons, a great achievement by the youths at the club.

12 - ACROSS THE WATER 1975-1976

Life at this time could not have been better, I had met my now wife Venetia at a disco in town and we started going out together, a partnership that has lasted the test of time. Venetia was always nice to see of an evening when Town had had a bad day, she was always so kind and gentle, after a while you would have forgotten everything that had happened that afternoon or evening.

The 75-76 season kicked off in August with Town having had just recorded record season ticket sales following the success we had had the previous four seasons, everything at the club was rosy very rosy. 27,680 turned up for the first game of the season against Newcastle Utd and what a disastrous start against a team that had struggled very much the previous season, we lost 0-3 and everyone went out of Portman Road staggered at the result, including me and dad, but as usual dad would say "don't worry son we're too good for that to last for long". After a good point at Spurs, with a goal from my idol Viljoen we were to have another set back at Leeds with another defeat, this time 1-0, not a disaster but we sure had to get things on track as soon as possible and thankfully after a draw with Burnley and a good 4-2 home win against Birmingham we surely did. I was still not at this stage going to many away games, but this was to change in the future seasons when me and dad joined the supporters club, we did go to the odd away game but not as many as we were to later on.

The league cup draw was made and we were drawn away at Leeds, great, we lost 2-3 in front of a paltry crowd of 15,318 with Johnson and Hunter scoring the goals, another Wembley dream over but with our record in the league cup, it did not surprise me and I suppose with Europe, we were probably best off out of it anyway. The UEFA cup draw had been made and we were paired with Feyenoord from Holland, a crack side which was going to be very difficult to overcome, but first we had the task of overcoming a very strong Liverpool side in the league. Liverpool v Ipswich games were becoming the games everyone wanted to see and this season was to prove no exception. Me and dad always looked forward to these games and with nearly 30,000 inside the ground we overcame them again with goals from Johnson and Austin, a lovely way to go into the game with Feyenoord.

For a nice change we had been drawn to play the first leg away and after a very good professional performance we came away with a 2-1 win, thanks to Whymark and Johnson who were later to become England internationals. After a shock 1-0 defeat to Man Utd away, who we normally always beat, we were to come up against the other lot from over the border, Norwich. Local derbies were hard enough for Norwich at this time anyway and nothing was to change, as 35,077 saw Beattie and Hamilton score the goals for another 2-0 derby win. It was always so nice going down the pub (Red Lion) when we had beaten the enemy, especially seeing a good friend of mine Ian Clements who was a staunch City fan and taking the mick out him all night, along with Steedy. The league season was not bad, but we were getting the odd defeats along the way which were keeping us down the league just slightly, but not to worry as we had the UEFA cup to keep us going. The second leg with Feyenoord at home was a great footballing affair with the two teams intent only on playing football, the tie was sewn up with Woods and Whymark on target and another European trip for Town was setup. As we left the ground after another fine display I couldn't help myself at asking dad if it would be possible if it wasn't too far if we could go and watch Town in the next round away, his reply was "let's see son, let's just see who we get". As it happened we were to be drawn with FC Bruges, a club just across the water and so I asked dad again about the chance of going to see Town away in Europe, his answer was "yes", I couldn't believe it we were to be going over the water to watch the Blues, brilliant absolutely brilliant.

The next few weeks were to seem like a lifetime, but what with having to book our trip through the supporters club which included travel by coach to Felixstowe, the ferry, travel over there to the ground, tickets etc, the first leg again was at Ipswich and me and dad were just hoping we could build a lead up enough to take over there so we could really enjoy our trip. Town played exceptionally well on the night and goals from Gates, Pedellety and Austin secured a superb 3-0 win and we were to go home in the car thinking only of our trip and how comfortable it was to be, how wrong we were going to be proved to be. A couple of decent results 1-1 away at Man City and a 3-0 home win over Aston Villa set us up for our trip which was being played on bonfire night, November 5th, what a bang we were in for, little did we know it.

The second leg of the game against Bruges had arrived and myself and dad met up at Portman Road to catch our coach to Felixstowe. We arrived at Felixstowe Ferry Port at about 08:00am and set sail for Belgium. After a decent crossing we arrived in Bruges and caught our coach to the city of Bruges. We had a good look around the city and got ourselves something to eat and drink. There were a lot of Town fans over in Belgium, I would say about 2,000. We had got seating tickets in the side stand of the stadium and were very much looking forward to the game. I was very excited at the thought of my first away European game, and after the first leg at Ipswich never dreamt of what was to come. We played awfully on the night, defended like kids and deservedly lost 4-0, 4-3 on aggregate. Me and dad were absolutely shocked and didn't know what to say to each other it was one of the worst trips home ever, apart from the West Ham Semi Final, that is, we arrived home about 11am the next morning, and I was so glad to be back home, although we were going to take no end of stick, but I didn't care really.

After being slaughtered at work about the defeat, things didn't improve the following Saturday as we lost again 1-0 to Wolves at Molineux, the next four league games were drawn and we had to get back on track soon and we did. Leeds United, Arsenal and West Ham were beaten in the next four games and Robson had got the show back on the road after what had been a disappointing period for the club. Christmas had come and gone again, and the FA Cup was upon us again, now after last season everybody had got the cup bug and this season we drew lowly Halifax Town at Portman Road a game we should win and duly did with a 3-1 win and Mick Lambert getting a hat trick, the draw on Monday lunchtime drew us with Wolves again in round four at home a tie we were all looking forward to.

After a fantastic 3-3 draw at Anfield in which Whymark got two and Gates the other, we drew at home to Coventry before we took on Wolves in the FA Cup. Now after last season Ipswich fans were in a confident mood going into the FA Cup. Wolves were having a bad season and we were becoming one of the forces in Division One, there could only be one winner, or could there? Wolves came to Ipswich in front of 30,000 backed by a big support of their own fans and held Ipswich to 0-0 on the day and forced a replay at Molineux, a game I still believed we would win. We went to Wolves very much still the favourites but in front of a partisan Wolves crowd of 31,000 we lost 1-0 and the Wembley dream was over again, would we ever do any good in the cup? Who knows! All we had left in our season was to try and qualify again for Europe through the league. We were very much up and down for the next few games with 12 points coming from the next 11 games, a run which didn't look likely to get us into Europe at the end of the season. A superb gate of 33,438 turned up to see the visit of Man Utd, a game that everybody always looks forward to and I certainly was not an exception or even dad for that matter, we always relished it. I don't know what it was but the boys from Old Trafford seemed to always freeze when they stepped onto the hallowed turf and this season was to be no different. A first half goal by Lambert and two more in the second from Whymark and Johnson sealed an empathic 3-0 win and yet another two points off the reds. The usual antics from about 5,000 Mancs followed after the game with a lot of so called fans running amok through the town, scaring old people and children on the way, they really were quite appalling scenes to witness in those days.

The next three games Birmingham 0-3, Arsenal 2–1 and West Ham 4-0 set us up for a meaningless game with Derby on the last day and what a fiasco it was. It was like watching a game on a Sunday morning when nobody really cares who wins or loses. Ipswich defended like kids and with the help of a hat trick from Francis Lee Derby ran out 6-2 winners to round off what had not been a bad season but on the other hand had not been a brilliant one either.

FC Brugge Pennant

13 - SO CLOSE TO MY DREAM
1976-1977

With Hamilton already gone to Everton there was to be another big shock to the system with David Johnson going back home to Liverpool, I was very disappointed as Jonty had become a firm favourite of every Town fan, including myself and Dad, he was wholehearted and scored his fair share of goals into the bargain as well. The team was changing all the time now with Bobby wheeling and dealing over the past couple of seasons, with players like Cooper coming from Birmingham City for next to nothing and also players emerging from the youth team like Brian Talbot et al etc.

We started the season with Keith Bertschin up front with Trevor Whymark, now although Keith wasn't the worst player in the world he certainly was no replacement for Jonty, he scored the odd goal but he was not the answer. I said to my dear Dad we have to sign a centre forward to link up with the formidable Trevor Whymark, we most certainly did sign a tremendous centre forward and we will talk more about that later on. We started off the season with the visit of Spurs and we duly beat them 3-1 with Lambert scoring twice and yes you have guessed it KEITH BERTSCHIN getting the other, a decent goal to be fair to the lad. We got off to a decent enough start in 76-77 losing only 2 out of the first 10 games, but still the talk was of a quality centre forward and he duly arrived in October 1976, his name, you guessed it, the one and only Paul Mariner. Bobby Robson had a bit of a tug of war with WBA and West Ham Utd but he was only coming to one club, the great Ipswich Town FC. He came in and he fitted like a hand in a glove he partnered Trevor Whymark up top.

His debut was against Manchester United at Old Trafford in front of 57,416 and as usual we beat them 1-0 with a goal from Clive Woods, what a debut to have. Mariners home debut was against WBA and I as usual was standing up the North Stand with my dear old dad, 25,373 people saw the debut of all debuts, we won 7-0 and Whymark got four goals, Beattie got what could only be described as a ROCKET past Osborne in the West Brom goal, Wark scored as usual, but what a goal Mariner scored, he took it up on the half way line and the WBA defence just could not stop his power and pace, as he got to the edge of the North Stand penalty area he unleashed a WORLDIE that just tore into the postage stamp between crossbar and post, Paul Mariner welcome to Portman Road, what an entrance that was folks. Ipswich had now only lost 2 out of 12 games since the first day against Tottenham and we would go another 9 games before we lost at Spurs 1-0.

After Spurs we had 20 games to go in Division One and we only got beaten 9 times, winning 9 and drawing 2 in what was a fabulous third place finish behind Liverpool and Manchester City on 52 points P42 W22 D8 L12, 66 goals for and 39 against. UEFA Cup here we come AGAIN. In the cups it was short and sweet, we played Brighton in the League Cup home and away and lost 1-2 on aggregate. In the FA Cup we drew Bristol City and smashed them 4-1 with Mariner (2), Whymark and Gates on the score sheet. In round 4 we drew Wolves and what a game that was in front of 32,996 we were 0-2 down and Mariner pulled one back to make it 1-2 and then it all happened we were well into injury time and the ball was pulled across the face of goal and who was to turn up, none other than George Burley and he simply smashed it into the top corner, the North Stand went mental literally. So it ended 2-2 and we went to Molineux for the replay but sadly lost 1-0 in front of 33,686 fans.

14 - EVERY BOYS DREAM -
THE FA CUP FINAL 1977-1978

In a season where we were to finish up playing 58 games, i t turned out into what could only be described as a total fairy tale. We started off at home to the Arsenal and duly put them to the sword 1-0 with Geddis getting the goal, it was to start a run of 10 games including Northampton in the League Cup of only 1 defeat in the first 10 games of the season. We lost a couple in October to Forest and WBA before getting back on track with a 5-2 win versus Birmingham City - we always beat them. The season was for the first time under Sir Bobby a bit hit and miss and we lost more games in the league than I can remember for ages but we kept winning the odd game which was to make sure we would be okay come the seasons end.

After the Birmingham game we won only 4 games out of the next 13 running up to the new year, Man City, Aston Villa, Leicester and QPR being the only sides that we had beaten. Boxing day was to become a nightmare losing 0-1 to Norwich City, how on earth did we lose to them WE NEVER LOST TO NORWICH. Anyway the FA Cup third round is upon us and me and dad were hoping for a good draw, which we got, a trip to Cardiff City who in those days were below average at best, anyway we go to Ninian Park with high hopes of progressing to round 4 of which we had no problem at all with Paul Mariner scoring twice to send us through in front of 13,584 fans at Cardiff. We lost the next 2 games of the season to Man Utd 1-2 at home and Chelsea away 5-3 before playing our next FA Cup game a home draw verses Hartlepool Utd, we played very well on the day and won 4-1 with m favourite player at the time Viljoen netting twice, followed by goals from Mariner & Talbot in front of 24,207 joyous Town fans. We were in round 5 of the FA Cup, but we had to be careful with our results in the league as it was getting very nervy to say the least.

We played one game before we went to Bristol Rovers in the cup, Leeds United at home, 0-1, so really not good preparation for a massive cup tie. So off we went down to Bristol Rovers, the weather was atrocious in the South West, the pitch was frozen and it had been snowing loads - game off? No this was 1978, the referee said GAME ON, unbelievable it really was. Anyway to the game we had not played to the conditions at all well and found ourselves 2-0 down, but a certain Robin Turner, who hardly ever played really, scored a brace and we drew 2-2, we really were very lucky as Bobby Gould had a perfectly good goal rule out for offside, there you go swings and roundabouts as they say, remember we were totally mugged off at Stamford Bridge versus West Ham in that infamous semi final, thanks to a certain MR CLIVE THOMAS, what goes round comes round and all that folks!!!

The replay at Portman Road on the following week was a walk in the park on a decent surface and we beat them 3-0 with Mills, Mariner and Woods sending us through to round 6 when we should meet up with a club called MILLWALL away, say no more everyone. We played 2 more league games before the infamous cup tie at Millwall, Newcastle Utd away, of which we secured a very good 0-1 win in front of 22,521, oh how times change over the years with fickle football supporters, we then played WBA at home and drew the game 2-2 with goals from Mills and Wark, these were a welcome 3 points from the 2 games in our battle to stay away from the bottom three or four teams in Division One. It was now March and the game at Millwall was on everyone's mind especially mine as it was such a big game for the club and also for me and Dad as we so wanted to erase the memories of Stamford Bridge, 1975, that game against West Ham still haunts me to this day, and always will, we was robbed hook line and sinker that night, trust me everyone.

So off we set for the Old Den, Millwall, now we took about maybe 6 or 7,000 fans to the Den that day and I must admit i reckon only about 4,000 of the supporters were still in the ground at 5:20pm when the game eventually finished all due to horrendous scenes in the ground due to Millwall fans causing mayhem all over the ground. They was up their end, they were in with the Town fans they were everywhere, just hellbent on causing trouble, which they did to such a degree the referee took the players off the pitch a couple of times. Whilst all this was going on Ipswich just got on with playing their football and they totally outplayed the lions from start to finish. Burley scored a worldie from 25 yards, Wark, Talbot and a superb hat-trick from Paul Mariner sealed the win for the Blues, I can still see Mariner now celebrating in front of the Millwall fans as if to say, up yours you are not stopping me or my team mates from playing in another FA Cup Semi Final and so it was a 1-6 win at an incredible hard venue and we was Highbury bound to play WBA, oh how we all loved that, revenge for 1975 YES PLEASE EVERYONE. The semi final was all everyone was talking about now but Bobby Robson had other things on his mind like staying in Division One of the football league, we played 6 games between the Millwall game and the semi final, winning one, drawing three and losing two. The one win was on March 27th 1978 versus Norwich City, we won 4-0 and what a moral booster that was, not only 2 points but a superb display in front of 29,989 fans at a delirious Portman Road, Brian Talbot with two, Geddis and Mills scored in what was to be the perfect tonic before a massive game against WBA in a weeks time.

We lost the next league game at Man City 2-1 with Mariner scoring our goal that day, but we were accumulating just enough points to be able to concentrate on beating the baggies at Highbury. I went with my mates for this game and Dad went on the coach, it was an electric atmosphere at Highbury that day, we was up the famous Clock end that day and WBA had the North Bank end, it was so noisy in the ground everyone was totally up for it. We had a certain Clive Thomas refereeing, yes Clive bloody Thomas, the man who disallowed TWO Bryan Hamilton goals at Chelsea that night in 1975, thank you for nothing our dear FA. The game kicked off and we was attacking the North Bank end where the WBA fans were standing, we had only been playing a few minutes when a great cross came in and Talbot scored with the bravest header you will ever see, he and John Wile the WBA centre half clashed heads and Talbot eventually went off to be replaced by Lambert and Wile carried on like a wounded soldier with blood seeping from an awful incident, Talbot also, although the goal scoring hero had a very nasty cut to his head and duly watched the rest of the game. We were playing out of our skins and after about 20 minutes oh my lord we were 2-0 up when Mills had a tap in, the Clock end was on fire, trust me everyone. Half time came and we were firmly in the driving seat, Wembley bound until a moment of madness from Big Al, he handballed in the area and Mr Thomas awarded a spot kick which Tony Brown buried up the North Bank end, Cooper wasn't helped by the fact that the WBA fans were throwing coins at him as he was preparing to save the penalty. Cooper was arguably the best penalty saver in Division One but not on this occasion, he had no chance, so it was game on but Ipswich never buckled at all and continued to play the Robson way and were reward very late on when Wark scored up our end to send the Town fans delirious, we was Wembley bound for the very first time in our history, oh how we celebrated, in the ground, on the way home and eventually in the pubs back in Bury St Edmunds, me and my mates had headaches for ages after we had partied more or less all night into Sunday morning, great memories indeed, we were in the FA Cup Final and I could hardly believe it, it was such an emotional day, you wouldn't believe "Wembley here we come".

We had 6 games from when we beat WBA and the FA Cup Final, we won only one, drew two, and lost three, the worst being a 6-1 defeat by Aston Villa, a game where famously Viljoen had quite a falling out with members of the team and staff, a very sad end to a brilliant career of his I may add, Colin Viljoen was always one of my favourite players, but it is what it is and he was to play no part in the upcoming FA Cup Final a very sad day for me, but we just get on with it as we always have done, Wembley here we come everyone. Of course we were in the UEFA Cup in 77-78 as well, quite a successful campaign, we played Landskrona Bois in round one and went through 6-0 on aggregate, this was followed by Las Palmas, a tricky tie but again we went through, 4-3 on aggregate, having drawn 3-3 at their place.

The next time round we played the mighty Barcelona and what a night that was. Barcelona had an unbelievable squad which included the greatest player in football at the time Cryuff, Osborne was given the job of marking him and completely marked him out of the game. We won the game 3-0 in front of 33,663 fans a night I will never forget with goals from Gates, Whymark and Talbot. We then proceeded to go to the Nou Camp, Barcelona knowing one goal would probably see us through, but it was to be a long night, we lost 3-0 making it 3-3 on aggregate, so it went to penalties and we went out of the UEFA Cup in a horrible way, nothing worse than losing on penalties that is for sure.

The League Cup we went out in round 4 to Man City at home 1-2 with the goal scored by Whymark, from the penalty spot, we never seem to do very well in that competition at all.

So now all our thoughts were on May 6th 1978, at a place called Wembley Stadium, now I had been to Wembley before for home internationals with England and schoolboy internationals with the school but I had NEVER been to an FA Cup Final, oh the joy of waiting for the biggest game in Ipswich Towns history. I didn't go with my Dad, he went with my brother and they sat in the seats at Wembley. I went with my friends in a minibus from one of the local pubs in Bury St Edmunds, the Black Boy, the landlord made sure we had enough beer in the back and we duly made our way down to London. As you might think, we had had a skinful by the time we got there and when we first got out of the bus there wasn't an awful amount of people about as we had left so early. So we had a good look around Wembley Twin Towers and then found a place where we could have another few beers and something to eat, before we knew where we were the gates were open and in we went. We were up the tunnel end at Wembley and everything about the day was just as I had always imagine it, Wembley pitch which wasn't the best that day as we had had so much rain leading up to the game, but it was Wembley so who really cares 'eh.

The players came out and did their usual pre-match looking at the pitch and taking in all that was going on, it was LOUD, very LOUD trust me everyone. Anyway it was 2:50pm and out of the tunnel everyone emerged, two pristine looking teams with their tracksuit tops on. Ipswich Town on the back of our Super Blues track suit tops, it made you feel 10ft tall, trust me everyone. Mick Mills led the line behind a very very proud Bobby Robson, he had fulfilled a dream of his over 9-10 years of taking his beloved Ipswich Town to an FA Cup Final and how it was to become one of the greatest days of his life and ours. 3pm and its time to kick off, we were attacking our end, the tunnel end, which seemed a bit unusual but hey ho, it's the Cup Final who really cares. We started brightly and got better and better as the half went on. Mariner hit the bar when it was probably easier to score and Geddis had a great shot saved by Jennings, we went in 0-0 but I said to my great mate Jon Steed god knows how we are not winning this game and to this day I firmly believe they, Arsenal didn't know what hit them that day in May.

The second half began and to be honest it was just like the first half it was all Ipswich and surely it was just a matter of time, Wark hit the post twice, same spot on the post, and Jennings produced a worldie of a save from a Burley header was it really going to be one of those days, of course it wasn't we had other ideas surely and so it was to be. Clive Woods had the ball and played a lovely ball out to Geddis on the wing he totally skinned the full back and pulled it back where big Willie Young made a total hash of his clearance straight to Roger Osborne who drilled it past the great Pat Jennings, oh the scenes I can't tell you it was like you had ten birthdays on the same day, it was an unbelievable, an unreal feeling of emotion. Roger was all caught up in the emotion and had to be carried off, a true Suffolk hero, a Suffolk lad who had made all of Suffolk so, so proud, but we had a game to win and on came Lambert and we had only one scare when McDonald went through but was met by super Cooper who made the save. We had been brilliant from 3pm to 4:55pm when the referee finally sounded that final whistle and we had become FA Cup WINNERS for the first time in our history, what a feeling that was for a lad who had been supporting Ipswich since 1964 and all I used to get in the early days was stick at school but now my team was up there with the very best and how we enjoyed it you bet! So up Mick Mills and the lads went to collect the FA Cup and when they came down to do their lap of honour I was in tears, I never ever thought I'd see the day, but I had and memories of 1975 were out of the window, forget West Ham, we were the FA Cup winners 1978 and how we celebrated it went deep into the night and early Sunday morning I may say. We travelled home in the minibus and eventually got back to Bury St Edmunds at what ever time.

The next thing I knew I was on my way on Sunday morning over to Ipswich with Venetia to celebrate on the Cornhill, oh my, what a day that was, about 150,000 people all over Suffolk had come out for the day and it was so much fun, everyone was happy, it was the party of all parties, just such a great day. The players and Bobby Robson eventually made it to the Cornhill on the open top bus, I think most of the players were a bit worse for wear from the night before, who could blame them. When the manager and players finally got to the balcony of the Town Hall there was a sea of blue and white everywhere you could see it was tremendous to witness as a Town fan 100%.

The players sang their songs, we sang our songs and everyone was on cloud nine, Bobby Robson and Mick Mills did their speeches and the players were singing along with the fans especially Paul Mariner, Beattie and Wark, they were always good for a party those three. Eventually it all died down and we all, with very sore throats went home very happy, very tired, but most importantly we were all FA Cup Winners, the lot of us and I am as proud today as I was when we kicked off at 3pm that marvellous day in 1978, so proud we had won it, something that lot down the A140 can only ever DREAM OF and that's a fact (lol).

1978 was to finish the most marvellous year of my life because not only had we won the greatest cup competition in the world, I was later in the year, only two months later on the 29th July 1978 I married my dear Venetia, a marriage that is still ongoing 44 years later, Venetia is my rock and always has been, a truly lovely lady that has NEVER ever stood in my way of supporting my football club, for that Venetia I thank you very much and very much still do, she is amazing, thank you my darling, I love you so much, Colin xxxxx

Top - Colin prepares for the 78 Final, Middle – the FA Cup Winning
Team, Bottom – Eric gets ready for the Final.

15 - DOUBLE DUTCH 1978-1979

After a season that to be quite honest was sensational the 78-79 season was to turn out to be the real turning point of the club coming to the fore in English football, and of course on the European stage as well.

Bobby Robson went out and signed arguably the best passer of a ball I have ever seen in Arnold Muhren and later in the season he went Dutch again by signing Frans Thijssen a totally different type of player, skill, great passer, good technically and fantastic clubman, he was simply the real package, thank you Bobby you really were a diamond when it came to transfers that was for sure.

Anyway back to the start of the season and we went up to the Hawthorns full of hope that this really as going to be our year but after losing 2-1 to WBA it was a bit of a wake up call really but West Brom were a more than decent side then so I suppose it wasn't all doom and gloom on the way home. We followed this up with a home game against Liverpool, this game famous to Town fans because this was the game that Muhren after we had lost 0-3 at home, went to Mr Robsons office and said boss this just isn't working, all the balls are going over my head all the time, and from that day forward Bobby Robson started coaching the team to go through the midfield all of the time, or as much as we possibly could, after that the football became sublime to say the very least especially later on when Frans Thijssen arrived from F.C Twente in January 79. As usual we had an awful time in the League Cup and went out in August to Blackpool 2-0, same old, same old I suppose everyone!

Anyway that gave Mr Robson time to adapt the team to our new midfield playmaker and after a difficult first few games it slowly started to tick. We beat Man Utd 3-0 with goals from Mariner (2) and Talbot, we really were starting to become a real pain in the rear end for Man Utd because we really were beating them nearly all of the time at this stage under Bobby. The next 12 league games produced only three wins, two draws and seven defeats but no need to worry as this was the time of the rebuilding process and we all trusted Bobby 100%. In the meantime we had started on the Cup Winners Cup journey and we drew AZ 67 in the 1st Round, we drew 0-0 over there and beat them 2-0 at Portman Road with goals from Mariner and Wark (pen). So our new European experience had got off to a great start, in September, we drew S.W. Innsbruck in Round Two winning 1-0 at home, Wark scoring again and we drew 1-1 over there with a certain Mr Burley scoring the goal would you believe. So we were okay in the Cup Winners Cup until March 79 and that was a while off and we could concentrate on the league than goodness.

After we lost at Old Trafford, yes you heard me right we lost 2-0, the tide was starting to turn big time after that game and turn it surely did everyone. From when we lost at United until FA Cup 3rd Round day we played 7 league games and we won four, drew one and lost two, the last being a 5-1 win over Chelsea with Muhren 2, Mariner, Wark and Osman scoring the goals, a perfect Christmas present for any Town fan at the time, that was for sure.

The FA Cup was back and of course we were the holders, we drew Carlisle Utd at home and they gave us a bit of a scare that day. We eventually went through, but it was close, we won 3-2 with Beattie, Muhren and Wark getting the goals. We beat Wolves 3-1 at home in the league on Jan 20th 1979 and so it was back to the FA Cup when we drew Orient at home, easy one may think, but no they defended really well and got a very good 0-0 draw. So it was off to Brisbane Road, I was elated as I had never been to Orient so that was more than okay with me.

We went to a cold Brisbane Road on the Tuesday of the next week and we duly won 0-2 with Mariner getting both, my god he was making a name for himself, he was an outstanding centre forward for the Town, the best certainly since Ray Crawford and that is saying something everyone. So the cup defence was going to plan and we drew Bristol Rovers at home which as far as me and Dad were concerned was excellent, we thrashed them 6-1 with Brazil 2, Mills, Muhren, Geddis and Mariner putting them to the sword and how it was a superb display and could and should have been more. It was February by now and Thijssen had signed and what an impression he made, he was simply awesome everyone. We played five games in the league before we had to play Liverpool at home in the FA Cup 6th Round. We won two, drew two and lost one, so we were handily placed in the table come the visit of Liverpool.

It was a cracker of an FA Cup tie played in front of 31,322 at Portman Road, these two teams along with Forest were the best in the country and what a tie it was. It was a game that you probably always knew one goal would decide it and that is exactly what happened with Dalglish scoring the winner just after half time, attack as we did we just couldn't break them down and our defence of the famous trophy was coming to an end, disappointing yes, but at least we went out to a top team and they certainly were that.

Three days before we played Liverpool in the FA Cup we had a certain Barcelona (YES BARCELONA NORWICH FANS) came to Town again in the Cup Winners Cup, 29,197 turned up to see our second successive win over that great club from Spain, we won 2-1 with little Eric Gates getting a brace, what a game he had, the atmosphere was electric and Cruyff went home with his tail between his legs again.

So before we were to travel again to the Nou Camp we had a couple of league games versus Coventry and Arsenal, we drew with Coventry 1-1 (H) and beat Arsenal 2-0 (H) so we travelled in good form and to be honest I really though we might turn them over because with Frans in the team anything is possible. We played the game over there in front of 100,000 barmy Spaniards and we lost 1-0, so we went out in the last eight of the Cup Winners Cup on away goals, that is what you call cruel everyone.

We came home and Town had twelve games to go, the first being at Anfield, now we hadn't got a very good record there and this season was to be no different and we lost 2-0 in front of 43,243 loud scousers, same old same old!!! The next eleven games were unreal. We didn't lose another game all season, winning eight and drawing three of our remaining games, a truly great end to a very very good season. We finished a creditable sixth in the league, so another season in Europe beckoned, thank you so much our dear Bobby and the boys, another fantastic effort by everyone involved indeed.

P.S I won't mention our visit to Wembley Stadium for the Charity Shield, oh alright I will, we lost to Nottingham Forest 5-0, told you it was not very good didn't I, a VERY BAD DAY at the office folks!!

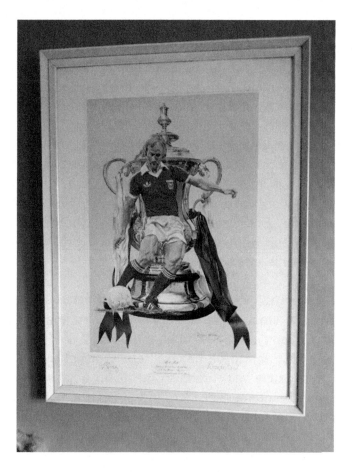

FA Cup Print with Mick Mills given to Colin by his Father in Law
Joseph Bright

Sir Bobby Robson – pictured with the FA Cup

16 - UNITED BROUGHT DOWN TO EARTH
1979-1980

After such a great previous season we started the league season of 79-80 in a total shambles, the first fourteen games we won 4, drew 1, and lost 9, yes nine folks, me and my dad just couldn't believe our start to the season, but as we kept saying it must get better because great players don't become average overnight and boy how we was proved right, BIG TIME EVERYONE!!!

Our League Cup adventure ended in Round Two as usual losing to Coventry City over 2 legs, same old, same old I hear you say (lol)! It was okay because we were in the UEFA Cup as usual and we drew Skeid Oslo and we had no problem beating them 10-1 on aggregate, 3-1 away and 7-0 at home, our next opponents were Grasshoppers of Zurich again like in Barcelona we went out on away goals, drawing 0-0 over there and drawing 1-1 at home, Beattie score but alas we were out, but at least we still had not lost at home in Europe ever "EVER NORWICH FANS"!!. After going out of the UEFA Cup we could concentrate on the league and my god how we played for the rest of the season was totally unbelievable, we were awesome, truly awesome.

Our last 28 games of the season we won 18, drew 8 and lost only 2, those defeats were to Coventry 4-1 and Man City 1-2 on the last day of the season. Those 18 wins out of 28 games in the top flight were against as follows: Derby, Southampton (twice), Bolton (twice), Spurs (twice), Man City, Wolves, WBA, Stoke, Bristol City, Everton, Palace, Leeds Utd, Coventry, Norwich City and last but no means least Manchester Utd. Now we left the last two to last for a major reason, anybody who is fairly young these days probably thinks we never ever beat Norwich City or Man Utd, but stop, you would be very wrong because anyone of my age and older would tell you that is far from the truth, we used to beat both of them regularly and that was home and away let me tell you everyone.

Anyway first of all we will talk about the Norwich game on April 5th 1980, 28,968 were in the ground and what a derby it turned out to be, John Wark got his usual goal, sorry goals against that lot, in fact he got a hat trick and Mariner got the other, they got a couple, but quite honestly we were in a different league from them and any HONEST Norwich City fan would totally agree, they were basically there to make the numbers up, so was their inferiority to the superb Blues, another trip down the A140 with your tail firmly between yours legs Norwich.

The other game we are going to single out is the game against Manchester United at home on March 1st 1980 in front of 30,120 supporters at Portman Road. Now this season United were having more than a decent season and came to Ipswich Town I think really fancying their chances, how wrong they proved to be everyone, oh yes, how wrong. Such was the big crowd me and Dad just for a change sat in the Lower Cobbold, that day and I remember it was a beautiful sunny day, well let's just say the sun was only shining down on Ipswich that day trust me. United turned us round that day and we kicked towards the North Stand first half, that's the first thing Martin Buchan (Captain of Man Utd) got totally wrong. Now you don't wind the Ipswich players up by doing a silly thing like making us kick the other way, trust me it will come back to bite you on the back side and bite them it surely did 100%. Paul Mariner hit the perfect hat-trick, Brazil got two and Thijssen got the other, so 6-0 but that's not the end of the story because during this 6-0 HAMMERING of that lot from Old Trafford we also had two penalties, one was taken twice and we also had another saved believe it or not by Gary Bailey the England goalkeeper who funnily enough was the son of Roy Bailey who played in goal for Ipswich Town in 1962 when we won the LEAGUE TITLE (Another one for you Norwich Fans, who haven't really ever won a lot). All in all a fantastic performance by an incredible team we had in those days, they were truly unbeatable on their day as United found out to their cost. United had a very good season in 79-80 and finished second, one place above Town who finished third, a great season when you think about the awful start we had, well done Bobby and thank you.

In the FA Cup of the 79-80 season we got drawn away to Preston in Round 3 and we won quite easily 3-0 with Mariner and Brazil scoring the goals, my first ever visit to Deepdale, a great historic ground is Preston. In round four we played Bristol City away and again it was my first visit to Ashton Gate, I remember standing up that open end as it used to be freezing cold in January with Dad, but at least we won 2-1 so that was good. Fifth round was against Chester with a very young Ian Rush playing for them, we won 2-1, but it was a struggle trust me everyone. Into the last eight and were up against Everton, again me and Dad went on the coach and stood up that silly end on the terrace low down, you could hardly see anything, we lost 2-1 and Beattie scored for us with a header after coming on as a substitute too little too late as we bowed out of the FA Cup at Goodison Park, oh well concentrate on the league as they say!

17 - CHAMPIONS OF EUROPE
1980-1981

By this time we were becoming one of the best clubs in Europe let alone England, Ipswich were fast becoming every fans second club, mainly because of the football we were playing, fast, controlled, brilliant passing side, we simply were fantastic to watch. I remember saying to Dad whenever am I going to match you and John (my brother) and see my club win the league and Dad said "don't worry it's coming, it's just a matter of time as we are the best team in the league". Well we were kind of, but we would never be seen as the best side until we had lifted that trophy for the second time, yes Norwich City fans we had already won it in 1962, but you know that really don't you!

The season started with a game at Leicester which we won 0-1 with a goal from Wark, a great start to what would become a memorable season. In the League Cup we did a tad better than normal and reached the 4th Round only to be knocked out away by Birmingham, we had previously beaten Middlesbrough and Norwich 1-3 at Carrow Road. I told you everyone we used to beat that lot in those days, sometimes more easily than others but on this occasion goals from Mariner (2) and Muhren was more than enough to send them packing. We were also involved in a UEFA Cup Campaign and oh what a campaign that was to become, we played Aris Salonika (Greece) in the 1st round and duly beat them 6-4 on aggregate, but after thrashing them at home 5-1 it was a different story in Greece and we had a game on for a while until Gates scored over there, eventually losing 3-1 but just doing enough to get through. We drew the side called Bohemians from Prague in the next round and again coasted at home 3-0 with goals from Wark (2) and Beattie, what a goal that was, thank you Kevin RIP my son, he was such an unbelievable player was Beattie, could do anything. So over to Prague we went for the second leg and again we didn't make life easy for ourselves losing 2-0 over there on a cold night but again our home form was enough to see us through, we were really starting to believe that this was to become an amazing season and how right we were proved to be everyone.

We were going great guns in the league at this time and by the time we played Widzew Łódź in the next round of the UEFA Cup we had played 17 games in our league season and had won 10, drew 6 and only lost one to Brighton, YES BRIGHTON, who finished 19th in the league at the end, I went to that game at the old Goldstone Ground and to be honest couldn't believe we had lost to them, but hey ho, onwards and upwards as they say. Just before we played the team from Poland I had been up to the City Ground at Forest to watch us beat a very good side 1-2 with goals from Wark (pen) and Brazil. They were a very good side in the early 80's and any win up there was a good win, trust me everyone.

So on to Round three of the UEFA Cup versus Lodz, now this side were a very good team and had just put Man Utd out of the competition but they hadn't bargained for what they were going to come up against at a noisy Portman Road, oh no! We went at them from the off and some of our football that night was an absolute joy to watch, we simply outplayed them and goals from Wark (3), Brazil and Mariner was enough to win 5-0 at a canter, job done as Bobby Robson would often say bless him. The second leg was played on a frozen pitch in Poland with Kevin Beattie wearing a short sleeved shirt, only Beattie would even think about doing that, but there again this was Kevin we are talking about, god bless him. We lost 1-0 and went through 5-1 on aggregate a fantastic result against a super team, last eight here we come everyone, more on that later in March 1981.

From the time we played Lodz at home until we first ventured our normal stab at winning the FA Cup we played 6 games in the league winning two, drawing three and losing one, the game we lost me and Dad ventured down to White Hart Lane and what a game we witnessed. It was end to end and we finished up losing 5-3 but it was totally mental as regards a proper game of football, every time Spurs or Ipswich went forward you always thought somebody would score it was just that kind of game, we came out of White Hart Lane a bit jarred off, but like Dad said to me "son this is a side capable of winning any league despite our defeat". I kind of knew what he meant, we were sensational as a team, but would we win it, time would only tell everyone. By the time third round FA Cup day arrived we were having a right ding dong with Villa in the league, we had already beaten them once in the league at Portman Road with Thijssen getting the all important goal for us to win 1-0 at home in front of 23,192 delighted Town fans. For the FA Cup tie a crowd of 27,721 turned up to see if we could put them out of the FA Cup as well, we won 1-0 with a great finish by Mariner up the North Stand end, I can still see his celebration now, arms aloft towards his adoring fans, the final whistle blew and we were in the 4th Round, would that be of more benefit to Villa, only time would tell, we were just elated to still be in the FA Cup, a competition that was adored back then, everyone wanted to win it, unlike now!!

It was back to league action now and my word were we on fire or what, in the next 11 league games after we played in the cup we won nine, drew one and lost one, the only defeat being to Man Utd at Old Trafford 2-1 with Butcher scoring our goal in front of 46,685 delirious Manc's, oh well, onwards and upwards eh! Utd were not in our class that season but hey ho!

In between those eleven games we had some massive cup ties, in the FA Cup we played Shrewsbury at Gay Meadow, my first visit there and what a quaint ground that was with the river running behind with a man in an oracle outside awaiting the ball if it went into the river. We drew 0-0 and Burley got a very nasty injury which was to see him on the side lines for ages. 18,000 packed into the ground but then everybody wanted a piece of Ipswich Town trust me everyone. We won 3-0 at home with Gates getting two and Wark scoring as well in front of 27,543 at Portman Road. We played Charlton at home in Round Five and to be fair to them they gave us a good game, Derek Hales and all, we won 2-0 with Wark and Mariner scoring in front of 30,221 and that was for a second division team, everybody loved Ipswich Town, everybody wanted to watch us full stop. It was lovely still being in the FA Cup but boy was it taking its toll on the players we only had a squad of about

16 players and what with the amount of games we were playing it surely was going to catch up with us, but we plodded on injuries and all and still went head to head with the VERY best anyone could throw at us.

March was here and the UEFA cup was back on the scene and we got drawn to play the great St. Etienne first leg away for a change, so I said to Venetia, I fancy going to that game and so I did, what an adventure that was. I went over on the ferry and got the coach down to St. Etienne it was about 12 hours on the coach, my god was I tired by the time we got there. On the day of the game all the French fans were blowing their car horns and sounding anything and everything, it was absolute mayhem, you couldn't hardly hear yourself think it was so loud. Anyway we finally got into the ground of which we was put in with the St. Etienne fans behind the goal at the front near the corner flag, more about that later everyone.

The game kicked off in front of 42,000 loud, fanatical St. Etienne fans and the noise went up ten fold when Rep put them in front, but to Towns credit we just went up two gears, we really did and we tore into them. Mariner got two brilliant goals, one a fantastic header, Muhren scored a superb shot and Wark got his goal as usual in the UEFA Cup. We had beaten one of the best teams in Europe on their own patch 1-4 and I still say to this day that was one of the greatest if not the greatest ninety minutes I have ever witnessed as an Ipswich Town supporter, I personally don't think it will ever be surpassed in my lifetime, truly brilliant from start to finish and all that on an awful pitch, it was like a ploughed field everyone, please trust me.

The journey home although very long seemed to fly by because of what I had just witnessed but home I got and my next focus was on to the following Saturday and a smaller trip to the City Ground against Nottingham with my Dad for another cup tie, this being a 6th Round FA Cup with Forest, another daunting fixture, in which was becoming an amazing season, onwards and upwards everyone. We went up on the coach and when we got there all we could see was a sea of blue and white. I suppose there must have been at least 6,000 Town fans at the City Ground, we were up the Bridgeford End which in the 1980s was an open end of terracing, superb for an FA Cup tie between two very, very good teams. Town were attacking our end first half and we totally dominated the early exchanges and before we knew where we were we were 2-0 up thanks to goals from Mariner and an Anderson own goal, we were flying as usual but Forest had other ideas and they fought their way back into the game and completely turned the game on it's head and scored three times to lead 3-2. Town were NEVER EVER dead in those days and Thijssen scored up the Trent End to send us home ecstatic with a 3-3 draw, trust me that was a superb score at Forest back then it really was. We replayed against Forest on the Tuesday night in front of 31,060 joyous fans and we were to be treated to a marvellous Muhren goal past the great Peter Shilton to win it, a fantastic atmosphere and a superb performance, semi-final here we come, Wembley Stadium bound, who knows I certainly thought we were.

As a club Ipswich Town were on everyone's lips, we were fast becoming not only the best team in England, we were ripping it up in Europe as well, we had beaten the best teams anywhere in Europe with some of the best players in Europe to boot, we were simply on fire! But as the games passed by we were suffering very much from injuries and it was to play a big part in the season's run in. In the league from March 31st we played Leeds Utd away and lost 3-0, we played another seven league games and only won 2, drawing 0 and losing five a devastating end to a league season that was so so good up until then. The hammer blows were a defeat at Norwich when we lost 1-0 literally two days before we played FC Cologne away in the Semi Final 2nd leg of the UEFA Cup, it was a fixture like no other, trust me everyone.

We had already beaten Cologne at home 1-0 thanks to Wark and we went to Germany under immense pressure and sealed a 1-0 win thanks to Terry Butcher, a fantastic achievement when you consider how many games we were playing which seemed like every day. So we were in the UEFA Cup final, an absolutely brilliant achievement by a club of our size, but we were there on merit and everyone was looking forward to the final. In between all of this we were still fighting hard to win the title and when we went to Aston Villa and won more or less a title decider 1-2 at Villa Park I really thought I was going to live my dream of seeing my team win the league, but it was not to be, like I said that defeat to Norwich, followed by an awful defeat at Middlesbrough (14th in the table) after being 0-1 up with a goal from Mariner as well, we lost 2-1 and it was making us even more sick when we heard Villa were losing 2-0 at Arsenal, a very sad day indeed, title dreams out of the window again, oh well, next season and all that folks! Believe it or not we played our last game of the season at home to Southampton on a Tuesday night exactly one week after the 1st leg of the UEFA Cup Final at Portman Road, absolute madness, it would never happen now, well at least I would certainly hope not folks. We had also lost an FA Cup semi final 1-0 to Man City at Villa Park, a game I just want to forget thank you!

UEFA CUP FINAL PORTMAN ROAD, MAY 6th 1981 - 27,532 VERSUS AZ67 ALKMAAR (HOLLAND)

Now because of all of the disappointment over the last few days or weeks what more could you want than a chance of becoming one of the BEST TEAMS in Europe, yes please I hear you answer, and that is exactly how I felt I had had my dream shattered by Norwich and some Yugoslav who scored twice for Middlesbrough, so now it was time to save our season and save our season we did, god only knows how we found the energy, Bobby, the players, the staff, fans or anyone we had just played 63 games and were just about to embark on our 64th with one league game to come, we would eventually play 66 games in one season and Russell Osman played in every game, a truly remarkable record, hats off to you Russell Osman,

I remember travelling over with Dad in the car and saying to Dad how many do you think will be in the ground tonight and we both agreed on about 34,000, so it was a shock to see only 27,532 in attendance, why I'm really still not sure because we always got over 30,000 for big games back then, always, it was a mystery to me and Dad. I remember the teams coming out together side by side and feeling so much pride, my club in a European final such a marvellous feeling. We started on the front foot and NEVER took our foot off the pedal, the lads were on a MISSION and how!! From when we were awarded a blatant penalty, scored as usual by Wark, we dominated from start to finish, with further goals from Thijssen and Mariner to finish up winning 3-0 and go into the 2nd leg with what looked like an unbeatable lead, more about that later. The players had done themselves, Bobby and the fans proud so now it was a wait of 14 days until the 2nd leg in Amsterdam at the Olympic Stadium, oh how you wish your time away sometimes, I certainly did, I just couldn't wait to board the ferry across to Holland.

UEFA CUP FINAL OLYMPIC STADIUM, MAY 20th 1981 - 28,500 VERSUS AZ67 ALKMAAR (3-0 UP)

I travelled over with friends of mine and what a couple of days we had, it was warm when we got over there and we met up with loads of Town fans and also quite a lot of servicemen who came up from Germany to support us because we were British. There were Leeds fans, Liverpool fans, in fact fans from all over coming to cheer us on, which I thought was superb to be honest everyone. We went to bars all over the place in Amsterdam and everyone was having a great time enjoying themselves in the lovely Dutch sun, there were even squaddies diving in the canals, brilliant, superb atmosphere 100%.

After what had seemed an eternity on the beers it finally ticked over to the time to go into the Olympic Stadium Amsterdam, we were up the end behind the goal, an open end of terrace in the full sun and my was it hot, even at kick off time. We started really well and scored early, this was going to be a walk in the park "Was it Colin??", no it wasn't AZ67 were a very good side indeed and they just bombed forward at will, they had nothing to lose at all, it was a game like Bobby said, like a game of basketball, one end to the other. Wark and Thijssen scored for us, but like I say AZ67 just kept coming at us and eventually scored four times, thank god we had that three goal buffer from the first leg at Portman Road, it was to prove pivotal that lead. The referee eventually blew the final whistle much to the delight of myself, my mates and all of the Ipswich fans. We were the Champions of Europe and how we celebrated, long into the night and the next day and the next day as well, we were in heaven.

Me and my friends got the coach and ferry home and when we finally arrived back in Suffolk I remember I went and bought the Sun newspaper and there it was inside the sports pages, Ipswich Town UEFA Cup Winners, it was then and only then it started sinking in to what my favourite football club had actually achieved, a lovely moment in the life of a true football fan, beautiful in fact. My lovely Dad didn't go to the final in Amsterdam, don't ask me why, I really don't know the answer everyone, but what I do know I couldn't wait to get home and see his face on;y I had got home to see my wife Venetia first, that was lovely. The next port of call a few days later was to go again to the Town Hall to see the homecoming and what a homecoming it was to everyone.

Again there were Ipswich Town fans everywhere just like when we won the FA Cup, on top of pubs, on top of roofs, on top of cranes, they were everywhere in the Town centre. The players again were in an open top bus and again most of them seemed a little worse for wear, but who cares, it had been an unbelievably long hard season now it was time for EVERYONE to let their hair down, and let it down we most certainly did. Wark, Mariner, Beattie the usual clients were in good for singing and dancing on the balcony with also Bobby Robson joining in as well with his jigs, songs and fantastic words for all us fans, along with Mick Mills who hoisted that magnificent trophy up high for all of us to see. It was great to see Alan Brazil had actually found his clothes after going up to pick the trophy up with the other lads in a certain white dressing gown (lol) in Amsterdam.

The celebrations went on all afternoon and long into the night in Ipswich Town centre, we were celebrating a truly magnificent Ipswich Town team that probably would never be seen again in a very long time, I and every other Town fan of the time were very lucky, I know that and I thank everybody that represented the club that season as we were brilliant from the Leicester City game up until May 20th 1981 when it all came to a massive climax.

Ipswich were voted THE BEST TEAM IN EUROPE IN 1980-1981 (By UEFA)

RUNNERS UP IN THE LEAGUE
FA CUP SEMI FINALISTS
JOHN WARK WON PLAYERS PLAYER OF THE SEASON
FRANS THIJSSEN WON WRITERS PLAYER OF THE SEASON

Says it all folks, I think you will agree (John Wark was my player of the season)

Frans Thijssen, Arnold Muhren, Colin and Eric with the UEFA Cup

Ipswich Town Players Coach

Colin pictured with Russell Osman, Alan Brazil and John Wark at Paul Mariner Day at Portman Road

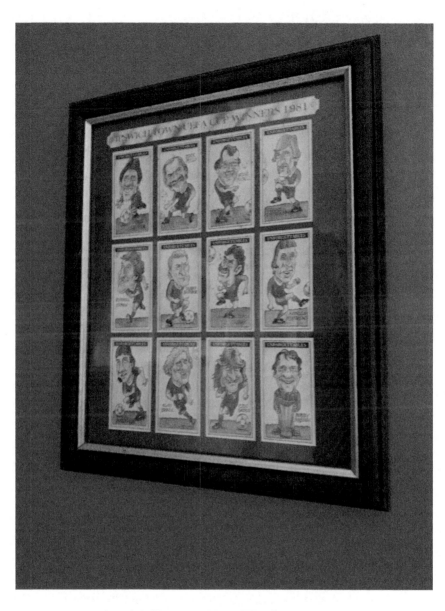

Ipswich Town – 1981 UEFA Cup Winners

18 - COULD WE GO ONE STEP CLOSER PLEASE IPSWICH TOWN FC 1981-1982

Season '81-'82 started just the same as usual with Town on fire and really, just carrying on from where they had left off the previous season, we were fresh after a long previous hard season and right ready to hopefully at long last lift that 1st Division title for the first time since 1962. The very first twelve league games only saw us beaten twice to Everton and Southampton both away, I may add, we won eight, drew two and it got us off to a superb start, just what me and Dad had prayed for indeed.

The Southampton game was my first visit to the Dell and what a game, we lost 4-3 with Wark getting two and Mariner getting the other in front of a packed 22,552 fans in the Dell. Okay, we lost but what a game that was and still is one of the best attacking games I have ever seen in the top flight, maybe apart from the Spurs game a few seasons earlier. The League Cup, a competition we still hadn't won, which got me a little bit because we obviously had a team capable of winning anything, but the trophy has always eluded us and still does. We drew Leeds Utd in the 2nd Round and beat them in both legs to go through 4-0 on aggregate, they really quite honestly at this stage were not in the same postcode as us, I remember they finished third bottom that season and were duly relegated I believe.

Our next two league games were Swansea at home and Stoke away, now with no disrespect Swansea and Stoke should not be taking points off us, but this is football and it's a funny old game as Greavsie once said. Swansea were a decent side having just got promoted and had a swagger about them, they came to Portman Road and won 2-3 a result along with the Stoke result that was to prove decisive in the title race. We lost 2-0 at Stoke, a side that was to finish 18th in the table, say no more, a real body blow to our title hopes, we just had to pick it up and we certainly did as the games went on trust me everyone. Of course we were the holders of the UEFA Cup and our defence of the trophy didn't go well at all, we were drawn against Aberdeen managed by Alex Ferguson, now that seemed a perfect draw, how wrong we would be proved to be. The first leg was at Portman Road and we drew 1-1 with Thijssen scoring our goal, now I and every Town fan thought we would still be okay at Aberdeen, but oh no we just weren't at the races that night and we lost 3-1 going out 4-2 on aggregate, a real body blow as holders but like I said to my Dad that would probably turn out to be a blessing in disguise, only time would tell as they say folks!

The League Cup had started late this season and in November we drew Bradford City at home, somehow or other City got away with a 1-1 draw so we had to replay at Bradfords home and they forced extra time before we eventually went through 2-3 with goals from O'Callaghan, Muhren and Turner. We drew Everton in round four and just for a change we were doing okay in the League Cup, we won 2-3 at Goodison Park, with Gates, Brazil and Wark on the scoresheet, a great win away from home. After the Stoke defeat in the league we were to go on a four straight winning run, Man City, Middlesbrough, Birmingham and Coventry City all beaten which got us well back to the title hunt once again. We had another home draw in the League Cup against Watford in the quarter finals and beat them 2-1 with goals from Wark and Brazil, we were in the semi finals, could we do it!?

After Watford in the League Cup it was back to league action and me and Dad couldn't believe we lost to Notts County at home, we had demolished them at Meadow Lane 1-4 earlier in the season at ease, but here we were at Portman Road losing to them 1-3, quite a shock to say the least. The League Cup last four had us paired with Liverpool over two legs, now everyone was saying whoever wins this tie will win the trophy and I certainly didn't disagree with that at all. The first leg was at Portman Road and we didn't turn up and got beaten 0-2 at home, so we had it all to do at Anfield certainly, but we were Ipswich Town, anything was possible and we lived in hope, even if only slightly at this stage. Believe it or not we had a league game at Anfield right bang in the middle of the two legs so we had to play there twice in three days, not good I hear you say! Well the game in the league was a chance for

Liverpool to avenge a 2-0 defeat at Ipswich and avenge it they most certainly did, they won 4-0 in front of 41,316 noisy and partisan scousers a defeat that might just cost us the title, who knows? The second leg of the Semi Final was a close encounter between two very good sides and Ipswich at least saved face on the night with a 2-2 draw, finally losing 4-2 on aggregate, so Liverpool marched on to Wembley and our awful League Cup run goes on for another season at least.

Just before the League Cup we had our annual tilt at winning the FA Cup and it all started very well at Birmingham where we won 2-3 with goals from Brazil (2) and Wark, we then went on to Luton Town away where we took loads of fans standing on what was the open terrace behind the goal. We played very well that day in the cup and eventually came out of the tie 0-3 winners, the only problem was big Terry Butcher sustained an awful nose injury that day there was blood everywhere. He was taken to hospital where he stayed for several days, I believe. Bobby Robson visited him all the time I was told, good old Bobby, one of THE VERY BEST in the game. After this tie I was saying to my Dad perhaps thi is our season again to win the FA Cup? How wrong I was, we drew Shrewsbury again away, and did we show the right attitude, well you tell me, me and Dad went on the coach to watch what we all thought would be a walk in the park, far from it Shrewsbury, with Gay Meadow filled to the rafters with 13,965 inside, had other ideas. They battled and fought for every ball as if their lives depended on it and duly beat us 2-1 in a game they deserved to win. D'Avray scoring our goal, the next day in the papers we were shot to bits by the press, and really we quite deserved it, it was a shock result, a BIG SHOCK.

Three days later and it was back to the league and boy how we responded, Southampton were at Portman Road on the Tuesday after the Shrewsbury game and we ripped them apart with Alan Brazil getting all five goals in a 5-2 win, simply unbelievable finishing from a superb number ten striker, that was the catalyst for us to go on an unbelievable run of only five defeats in the last twenty two games, 14 wins and three draws that includes the

Southampton game folks. So those earlier defeats to Swansea (H), Stoke (A) and also Wolves (A) (2-1) who finished second bottom and we relegated, really cost us dear, well those results cost us the title they really did, always next season I suppose! RUNNERS UP AGAIN!

	P	W	D	L	F	A	Points
LIVERPOOL	42	26	9	7	80	32	87
IPSWICH TOWN	**42**	**26**	**5**	**11**	**75**	**53**	**83**
MANCHESTER UNITED	42	22	12	8	59	29	78

Pioneer Stand Improvements

19 - A DIFFERENT BOBBY (NOW)
1982-1983

After another incredible season of so close and yet so far the inevitable happened, now Bobby Robson was wanted and turned down some of the biggest names in English football, but when England come knocking you have to have a very good think about it and obviously Bobby did and he decided in his own wisdom this was a job he just couldn't turn down, and to be honest most of us would have done the same thing as Bobby Robson. He had been at the club for the best part of thirteen years and gave it everything, from myself and every Town fan especially of that era, thank you Bobby for everything and more importantly thank you for making our club and making us happy almost every day you were here, you will be remembered at ITFC forever. Now Mr Robson had a coach called Bobby Ferguson another Geordie who was hard as a rock, I believe he never suffered fools gladly, possibly the ideal replacement for Mr Robson, time would tell.

By this time the ground was changing, we had a new or kind of new West Stand where the club was putting another tier on to the old stand. It was positive, thinking, yes, but it cost us dear in the months and years that followed, trust me everyone. We started the season not too bad, in the first five games we drew three and lost two, those two being 1-2 at home to Spurs and 3-1 at Man Utd. So no wins, but a steady start I suppose. In the UEFA Cup we were drawn to play Roma and the first leg was in Italy, now going to Italy anytime is difficult but especially when you have not won one game yet in the season. We lost 3-0 in front of 60,334 crazy Italians, not the best start of the season for Mr Ferguson I would suggest!

So we flew home from Italy on the back of a 3-0 defeat, what's best, yes you have guessed it a home game in the league against Stoke City, well it would have been if we hadn't lost 2-3, oh dear, three points out of eighteen, pressure on already Fergy. What Bobby Ferguson needed was a fairly comfortable game in the league to get the side firing and he surely had that coming up at Meadow Lane, home of Notts County. I went to this game because I hadn't been to Notts County before, tick the ground off and all that. Anyway we proceeded to tear them apart, fantastic football, superb passing and we won 0-6 with goals from Mariner (2), Brazil, Wark, Thijssen and McCall, was this the start of a revival well time will tell, but it certainly was a very good team performance, brilliant at times. We played Liverpool next in the league and this fixture was always massive between two exceptional clubs, we won 1-0 with Mich D'Avray scoring the winner at Portman Road, surely this was the tonic we really needed.

The League Cup was here again. We drew Liverpool in round two, oh well, off we go again against the mighty reds. We were at home in the first leg and lost 1-2 and lost 2-0 at Anfield, 4-1 to Liverpool on aggregate, bye bye League Cup AGAIN!!! We were not doing very well really in the cups because we had already gone out of the UEFA Cup despite a fantastic 3-1 win at home to Roma we went out 3-4 on aggregate, at least we still maintained our unbeaten European home record, not many teams can say that can they, especially because we have faced THE VERY BEST teams in the whole of Europe at Portman Road since 1962.

After we had lost 0-1 at home to Arsenal in October we then went on a decent run of only one defeat in the next nine games, winning five, drawing three, it got us back on track a bit and away from the struggling sides at the bottom. It was a funny season really because we were very stop start and we lost our next three games against Everton, Watford and at Christmas on the 27th December against Norwich, Osman and Mariner scored against Norwich City in a 2-3 defeat, oh how the turkey tasted crap that Christmas, two days later we headed to Villa and got a 1-1 draw followed by a 2-1 win versus Southampton on New Years Day, so all in all not too bad a Christmas I suppose.

Everyone looks forward to the FA Cup at Christmas time and on Jan 8th we played Charlton at home, a game we won but made a meal of winning 3-2 with goals from Thijssen and Wark (2) to put us through, my goodness we needed the FA Cup this season with our up and down League form, that was for sure folks. Again our next two games before the 4th round of the cup were against

Brighton at home which we won 2-0 with Wark and Brazil on the scoresheet, followed by a defeat to Stoke City away 1-0, my goodness do we ever win at Stoke? This led us into playing Grimsby in the cup and we had no problems at all, beating them 2-0 and into the fifth round where we were to come up against a certain club called Norwich City at Carrow Road. We played two massive games in the League prior to our visit to Norwich, drawing 1-1 at home to Man Utd and losing 1-0 at Anfield against Liverpool, we were handily placed in the League so no real worries going into a massive 5th Round FA Cup tie with the enemy, as they say.

Now, my birthday is on February 18th the same day as Bobby Robsons, and what day should we play Norwich, February 19th, so although not on my birthday, what a post birthday present that would be, to beat that lot and proceed into the last eight of the FA Cup. Well that's where the dream ended as we went there quite confident but got beat 1-0 in front of 28,001 fans at Carrow Road, not a present I will remember for too long, trust me everyone.

After the debacle that was Norwich in the cup, we had fifteen League games to go and we finished quite well with six wins, five draws and only four defeats, so a sound finish to an average kind of season. Verdict on Bobby Ferguson's first season in charge, not bad at all really, an unbelievable task of taking over from a man of the calibre of Bobby Robson, well done Fergy! (9th PLACE IN DIVISION ONE)

20 - EVER CHANGING FACE OF IPSWICH TOWN 1983-1984

Since 1980 the club had seen Woods, Hunter, Muhren, Brazil, Mills and Thijssen move on, could this get worse, of course it could later in the season Paul Mariner and the great John Wark were to leave the club, all because of one expansion to the main stand, what a disaster that was going to become in the months and season ahead! We brought a couple of players in notably Romeo Zondervan, a Dutchman from WBA and also Alan Sunderland from Arsenal who funnily enough had played against us for Arsenal in the 1978 Cup Final. Zondervan was a great signing, full of energy, great ball player and a never say die attitude, just what the doctor ordered really, to sum it up two decent signings, but to be honest, were they as good as what we were getting rid of, of course they weren't but better than some others of course everyone.

We still had a decent First Division side but it just wasn't the same especially after Wark and Mariner were sold, but the show must go on as they say and we opened up the season with a game against Spurs, a game which we won 3-1 with Gates and Mariner on the scoresheet again, my god what a player little Eric Gates was, he was always such a favourite of my Dads was Gatesy, tremendous shot on him for such a small lad.

Bobby Ferguson was not doing a bad job really at the time, and we got off to a decent start to the season in '83 to be fair, winning versus Spurs and then going on a little run of three wins and a draw in the next four games, including a great 5-0 win versus Stoke, a game I remember vividly for Warks celebration, arms aloft as he wheeled away up the Churchmans end, good old WARKY!! The Football League Cup was to be another season of what might have been, and after wins against Blackburn over 2 legs and QPR in Round 3, we were to go out again to Norwich in a cup competition 0-1 at home, the less said the better I would suggest everyone, this cup was just not to be for Ipswich Town again!!!

The League season was to be a bit of a struggle, but we kept picking up three points here and there and keeping our heads above water thank goodness. Between September and December 26th we really had quite a struggle, fourteen League games only produced three wins, three draws and eight defeats, the highlight being a 1-0 win over Arsenal with Gates scoring the goal, Boxing Day produced one of our better performances and we won 3-1 in front of 14,477 fans, the attendances were getting worse as we fought our way into a position of safety, hopefully everyone. The very next day was derby day against our neighbours from down the A140, it was not the best game in the world, between two sides desperate for the three points, it finished in a stalemate 0-0 in front of 25,679 at Carrow Road.

The FA Cup was to pair us with Cardiff City at Ninian Park, could it be an omen, well I went and it proved to all us fans that we were still very much a First Division side as we completely dominated the game and won 0-3 with Gates getting a well deserved hat trick. The omen of drawing Cardiff in the third round away didn't last in the FA Cup for long, we drew Shrewsbury (again) away of which myself and Dad went and we lost 2-0, a total embarrassment may I tell you, an awful result, terrible, out we go without a whimper!! Our next twelve games in the League were to become a nightmare, we won only two, drew none and lost ten, I remember saying to Dad my goodness we are in a relegation fight here and we really had to start getting results because we were in our worst position since 1978, but we did win the FA Cup that year, but this season we had no other distractions so perhaps we might be okay, we will see as they say.

Paul Mariner scored his last goal for Town against Coventry at home in that awful run of games and a certain Jason Dozzell scored THAT GOAL as well in that game at 16 years old, unbelievable. Wark scored his last goal (for now) against Liverpool at home with a penalty in November, quite a quirky piece of fate as that is exactly where later in the season Warky was heading. Like I said earlier, Alan Sunderland and Zondervan had joined the club and rather like when Clarke and Robertson joined us in the

1969-1970 season they were to play a great part over the last games of the season.

After a 0-0 draw at home to Watford, the last nine games were to produce six wins, two draws and only one defeat against QPR away 1-0. The wins were against Luton, Wolves, Norwich 2-0 (with Sunderland and Zondervan scoring), Sunderland, Manchester Utd and Aston Villa. The draw away at Anfield 2-2 against Champions Liverpool with Gates getting both was superb, as was the win AGAIN at Old Trafford, against Man Utd who finished fourth in the table, D'Avray and Sunderland scored the goals that saw us finish in a respectable twelfth place, especially after a buffer win on the last day at home to Villa 2-1. What at one stage looked like probably relegation to the Second Division turned out to be quite a good season, only Ipswich Town could do that to their superb group of fans everyone, Division One status secured, thank you Mr Ferguson, and especially Sunderland and Zondervan, two great signings indeed Bobby.

It was during this season on November 24th 1983, that we celebrated the birth of my first son Ian.

Colin pictured with Jason Dozzell – one of the youngest players to score (16 years and 57 days) in the English top flight

21 - THE STRUGGLES CONTINUE
1984-1985

Again changes were happening this coming season to the playing staff, two of our UEFA Cup winning squad left the club, Russell Osman was to sign for Leicester City and Kevin O'Callaghan went to Portsmouth, incomings were Grew a goalkeeper from Oldham and also Kevin Wilson joined from Derby County, what a good signing he was to prove to be.

The start of the season saw me and Dad travel down to West Ham for the season opener, it was a bit drab finishing 0-0 but we thought a point on the first day away in London was not a bad result, maybe it was, maybe it wasn't, time would tell. The next three games on paper were not easy, Luton at home, Man Utd at home and eventual Champions Everton away, we were to draw all three games all 1-1, although we had dropped eight points out of twelve, I thought it was decent against very good top flight sides, time would tell. The League Cup our not so favourite competition started in September and we demolished Derby County 5-3 on aggregate to setup a tie with Newcastle at home, we drew 1-1 and had to go up there for a replay, we came away with a 1-2 win thanks to D'Avray and Gates, maybe this was our year in the League Cup, who knows everyone.

Meantime in the League the next eleven games leading up to our next League Cup tie against Oxford United produced three wins, three draws, and five defeats, not a bad start I said to Dad, but not brilliant either, we had work to do, that was for sure everyone. The Oxford game was to prove difficult, but we went through 2-1 and everyone was starting to dream again. Was it our year, who knows? The next eight League games we really needed results to get us up the table, it was not to happen and we won only two, drew none and lost six, not very good at all, but every cloud and all that everyone. The wins were against Stoke away 0-2 and Norwich City at home on New Years day, a certain Jason Dozzell and Eric Gates getting the goals, my god how Jason celebrated, he was an Ipswich lad and scoring against the enemy was everything to him, but don't forget it meant everything to us as well, HAPPY CHRISTMAS NORWICH CITY FANS (LOL).

By now it was FA Cup 3rd Round day again, and believe it or not we were away to Bristol Rovers (again), but hey ho, just get down there, and do the job boys, we won 1-2 with goals from Dozzell and Brennan, a player I always liked a quality midfielder who could score a goal, just what we needed. We didn't play another league game in January leading up to a League Cup games against QPR, we drew 0-0 at home, but we had no problem at Loftus Road, winning 1-2 with goals from D'Avray and Zondervan, Wembley, we can dream eh! In between the two legs against QPR, we played Gillingham in the FA Cup and again they really pushed us at home, we won 3-2, but it was a lot closer than me and Dad ever thought it was going to be but hey ho, fifth round here we come, where we would be drawn to play Sheffield Wednesday at home.

In late February we had two massive League Cup Semi Finals over two legs against that lot down the A140 Norwich. The first leg was at Portman Road and we played superb on the day, but did not get the luck in front of goal we deserved. We won 1-0 with D'Avray lifting the roof off Portman Road, was it enough, only time would tell everyone. I so wanted to win the League Cup. Just before the second leg we had another massive FA Cup tie against Sheffield Wednesday at home in round five, Zondervan, Burley and Sunderland were to score the goals to see us into the last eight of the FA Cup again, this time away to top of the table Everton daunting yes, but its the FA Cup as they say anybody can win if their attitude is right, we all know that everyone, I said to Dad although we weren't really doing brilliant in the League maybe this was to be another year at Wembley, who knows, anything can happen in the cups, it was to become much clearer in the week ahead that was for sure.

The Norwich semi final second leg was to be played on March 6th with the sixth round FA Cup tie at Goodison Park on the Saturday the 9th March, thank you very much indeed the FA and Football League for nothing! Only 23,545 turned up at Carrow Road for a semi final of the League Cup, an awful attendance for such a big game, was it to prove their downfall, maybe not. Having played so well in the first leg we all went to Carrow Road feeling very good about ourselves, but it was to be a long horrible night in Norfolk believe me. We were always going to have a spell when Norwich were on top and after they scored the first goal I said to Dad, don't worry we will score at least one, which I thought would be enough to see us through to Wembley, how wrong I was, Steve Bruce came up for a set piece and powered a header in and that was that, we had to put up with all the abuse going back to the car, you know what I mean, it hurt, it hurt a lot, but hey ho, they were to go on to win a Milk Cup, but also got RELEGATED, what do they say, what goes around and all that folks. We had to lick our wounds and get on with a mouth watering sixth round FA Cup tie at Goodison Park against a team that was on fire in Division One of the Football League.

So off we went AGAIN for a quarter final tie at Goodison Park, we all hoped for a better result than we had in 1980, but remember this wasn't the same Ipswich team we had then, and Everton were flying. I said to Dad if we got a draw at their place we would be more than happy, and draw we did. Town played very well that day, defended brilliantly and scored goals from Wilson and Zondervan to set up a mouth watering replay at Portman Road on the following Wednesday. A very decent crowd of 27,737 turned up on the night half expecting a win that would take us through to our fourth FA Cup semi final, but it was not to be and a very good Everton side secured a 0-1 win to go through, no complaints really it is what it is everyone, another great FA Cup run by the lads full stop.

By this time we had a battle on in the League and we had to get our act together of which we most certainly did to a greater extent. We had seventeen League games to play of which we won seven, drew four and lost six, so not too bad at all everyone. The wins were against WBA away, Forest (H), Norwich (A), Spurs (H), Leicester (H), Stoke (H) and Sunderland (A) my first and only trip to Roker Park I may add they got relegated that season with

Norwich and Stoke City. The match at Carrow Road was funny, really funny because although they were struggling in the League the crowd was 18,227, yes 18,227 everyone still one of the lowest attendances I have ever witnessed home or away in an East Anglian derby game, probably the worst. Anyway to the game itself, we really owed the canaries one and how, we won 0-2 and took the mick out of the Norwich fans all afternoon, because we knew a win would probably send them down, later in the season and it did, lovely!! Butcher and D'Avray getting the goals. We were to finish 17th, but it was very, very close believe me to relegation, too close.

22 - 18 YEARS OF TOP FLIGHT OVER 1985-1986

Now was the time for nearly all our top stars to depart, most notably Butcher was to go to Rangers, Burley went to Sunderland and Putney was to cross the divide and go to that lot down the A140. Steggles also departed, he was to be sold to Southend United. Players who arrived were Ian Atkins from Everton, a very good signing in my opinion, Rimmer also came from Everton and Gleghorn a midfielder was signed from Seaham Red Star for probably a nominal fee one would suspect. As the headline suggests this was to be an awful season for the club, and the culmination of what had been three or four years of constant struggle with money matters mainly to do with the construction of the what was then called the Pioneer stand, we lost WORLD CLASS players left, right and centre, something no First Division club would have been able to handle, we certainly couldn't.

The first four league games were to set the tone for the rest of the season, we opened up at QPR and duly lost 1-0, we then played Man Utd at home and lost 0-1, we actually won our next game versus Spurs at home 1-0 but the next trip was to Anfield to face the eventual champions Liverpool and this was the game that really told me and Dad we were in trouble this season, we lost 5-0 and Liverpool won at a stroll, it was a very long afternoon, trust me everyone. The next four league games were to produce only one win, that was at the Hawthorns against WBA, two defeats and a draw and we had only picked up seven points out of the first twenty four, just not good enough for Ipswich Town FC, we knew it was going to be a long, long season as it was to prove everyone.

The League Cup was a good distraction from what was becoming an awful League campaign, we drew Darlington in round two over two legs and we duly despatched them 7-2 on aggregate with Wilson scoring five of the goals in the two legs, Yallop and Dozzell scoring the others, oh how nice it was just to see a couple of victories in what was a dreadful start to the season. The next six league games were a nightmare, we won none, drew one and lost five, the only point coming against Newcastle at home (2-2) with Zondervan and Cole getting the goals, my oh my what an awful season this was becoming, this worst I had ever seen really since I first started going in 1964. It was back to the League Cup by now thank goodness and we were to play Grimsby away, my first trip to their ground in front of only 6,684 fans we won 0-2 with Cole and Wilson getting us through to round four, my god its cold in Grimsby trust me everyone. It was becoming a tough season to stomach and me and Dad were both of the same opinion. If we didn't pick up points soon in the League we would be in almighty trouble and so it proved.

The next four league games leading up to the next round of the League Cup brought only one point that coming from a decent draw at Maine Road, Manchester with a Brennan goal, a game that I was at, we really were struggling for points and the three defeats were a real body blow, being against Chelsea (H), Everton (H) and a humdinger of a game 4-3 at Oxford, yes Oxford were a top flight side in '85-'86 believe it or not everyone. The League Cup was on us again and in round four we drew Swindon at home we beat them 6-1 and at a canter I may add, a fine win with Butcher 2, Cole 2, Wilson and Brenan scoring to put us into round five again, where we would meet Liverpool, oh no folks! The next seven league games up until New Years day we picked up and got some better results, we won three, drew two and lost only two against Man Utd and Spurs away, so all in all not a bad return rolling into the New Year.

The annual FA Cup draw had been made and we drew Bradford at home, lovely me and Dad said "was it", we drew 4-4 in an epic cup tie in front of only 13,003 fans, gates were really dropping off at this point because of a lack of consistent football being seen. We played Birmingham away before the replay and won 1-0 thanks again to Kevin Wilson who was fast becoming a real all round favourite, everyone loved Jockey Wilson up the North Stand. Up to Leeds we went on a cold night in Yorkshire to play Bradford, only because Bradford were not playing at home at the time due to the fire at their ground, we won 0-1 with Brennan netting, but I must say I felt really sorry for them because of what their club and fans had been through. We drew West Ham Utd in round four and it was to become a marathon of a tie, we were at Upton Park first and drew 0-0 in front of 25,035 the replay at Portman Road went to extra time with Dozzell scoring the Ipswich goal in a 1-1 draw again, a second replay was then played and we lost 0-1, that season was the 16th consecutive season Town had progressed past the third round of the FA Cup. Before that game we had an unenviable trip to Anfield in the League Cup fifth round in front of 19,762 fans. I can't remember ever going to Anfield with so few fans in, especially as they were flying in the League, a League they were to go on and win by the way, we lost 3-0 and never deserved anything out of the game at all to be fair, League Cup hopes over AGAIN everyone.

The last fifteen league games started with champions elect Liverpool and we found something extra that day and won 2-1 thanks to D'Avray and Wilson, we followed it up with another very good win against Forest 1-0 with Butcher scoring the winner, we had some hope at last everyone. The last thirteen league games produced only three wins, three draws and seven defeats, it was to be our lot in Division One, we took it right to the end but with lets say unusual results going on in other grounds over the country we were to be relegated out of the top flight for the first time since 1968, a great run of top flight football but from next season it was to be very much back to the drawing board of Division Two football. I couldn't believe it and neither could my Dad, but like we said we have just go to get on with it and get back to where we belong, however long it may take, and that is exactly what we did.

BYE BYE DIVISION ONE, we will be back whenever trust me everyone.

23 - 5th PLACE, GOOD BUT NOT GOOD ENOUGH 1986-1987

Bobby Ferguson was still our manager after relegation from the top flight, but for how much longer, only time will tell everyone. The crowds were getting smaller by the week and also the squad was completely different now compared to the previous seasons. We were even signing Norwich players now with John Deehan coming across the divide to Ipswich, a player I have to say I always rated, very good target man was Mr Deehan.

A crowd of only 12,455 watched our first home game versus Grimsby Town, it finished 1-1 with an inevitable goal from Wilson but was this to be the start of a promotion campaign only time would tell everyone, the next five games were to only produce eight points, so we weren't setting the world on fire but there again we had only lost one out of the first six games, so not all bad as they say. We drew Scunthorpe in the League Cup and beat them 4-1 over the two legs, Cambridge Utd was to follow at the Abbey Stadium my first ever visit, and not the best we lost 1-0 in front of 8,893 joyous amber and black fans, that League Cup I hear you say.

The next eighteen league games leading up to New Year saw us win nine games, draw four and lose five, it all equates to not really a bad first half of the season and promotion was probably just still on, if only by a thread, play offs were definitely still on that was for sure. The FA Cup was to become our first defeat in round three for ages, we lost 0-1 at home to Birmingham in front of only 11,616, oh how the times were changing and not for the better either everyone.

The last eighteen league games produced six wins, six draws and six defeats, a sequence that would see us into a play off with First Division Charlton Athletic, the first game at home was a 0-0 draw and the second leg, my first venture to the Valley was a 2-1 defeat with McCall scoring for Town, so Second Division we stay!!

My second son Andrew was born on February 14th 1987, another Town fan.

24 - ANOTHER FOUR LEGENDS DEPART
1987-1988

After playing for the Town for which seemed like a lifetime we were now saying goodbye to Cooper, a goalkeeper of pure quality, thanks for everything Paul, also we were saying goodbye as well to Steve McCall, an unsung hero if ever there was one, thank you Steve for everything mate. After a few games at the start of '87-'88 season we also said goodbye to goal-machine Wilson, thank you very much Kevin for everything mate. I leave the last one to last because Bobby Ferguson although always in the shadows of Bobby Robson was a legend of the club, he was youth coach, reserve coach, first team coach and also the manager, Bobby you had a totally unenviable job of following Mr Robson and you came up short, a lot of managers do, so I don't and won't blame you, you were a terrific club servant and I thought you did an okay job under the circumstances Mr Ferguson, we miss you and thank you.

So in came John Duncan, not everyone's choice, but as usual I was always willing to give a manager a chance, too big a club for him? Only time would tell everyone, he brought in Harby, Lowe and Woods and out went Atkins, Brennan, Cranson, Gleghorn and Hallworth, several of those players went later on in the season, at the near end of the season. Crowds were down and the football was not always the best under Mr Duncan, but hey ho we have to give him a chance.

The first eight league games produced three wins, three draws and two defeats, not a bad start under a new boss, but promotion had to be the aim at least this season. Our League Cup run this season was to start with a two legged tie against Northampton, we won 5-3 on aggregate to send us through, this was to be my first visit to the County Ground in Northampton, oh my god what an eye opener after watching games at Portman Road all my life (lol).

The eighteen league games up to New Years day were to bring ten wins, three draws and only five defeats, so John Duncan was not doing too bad at all really in his first season in charge of Town.

One of the highlights of that run was a super 3-0 home win over Man City, with Rimmer (2) and Harby scoring the goals for Town in front of 12,711 fans, that was how bad it was getting at Portman Road everyone. We had been in a competition called the Full Members Cup from the previous season, the less written the better, it was in my opinion a waste of time and money.

We played another couple of games in the League Cup beating Southend at home 1-0 before going out at home to Luton Town 0-1 in what could only be described as uneventful on the night in front of 15,643. It was FA Cup time again and we drew Man Utd at home, a game that was televised live and that wasn't very often in those days, Town played really well and were a tad unlucky to lose 1-2 with Humes scoring from a header if my memory serves me right, unlucky Town!

The last eighteen league games saw us win six, draw three and lose nine of which five of those losses were on the trot, not good enough if you are aiming at promotion, that is for sure everyone. We finished 8th and I suppose for a first season it was not too bad, but hey this is Ipswich Town we are talking about and we need promotion the next season or two it would prove pivotal to Mr Duncan to see whether he could handle it, we will see everyone.

25 - WELCOME MR BALTACHA
1988-1989

A certain John Wark had returned to the club the previous season but only played seven games, but now he was back to the fore and boy how we enjoyed seeing him back. David Linighan signed from Shrewsbury and Ian Redford joined from Dundee Utd, in short decent signings for the Second Tier of English Football. A certain Sergei Baltacha was to sign but not until around about Christmas time. Dalian Atkinson had come in the season before and really finished '87-'88 with a bang, 6 goals in his last 5 games, so we were itching to see him in action, also Simon Milton who had signed from my local club Bury Town, I so wanted him to do well and boy over the seasons to come he certainly did not disappoint at all.

We started the season remarkably well, in the first nine games we won six, drew two and only lost one, Atkinson was ripping it up and I remember saying to Dad surely this is going to be our season, but what we had to remember was there were some really big clubs in the Second Tier that season, Chelsea, Man City, WBA, Leeds Utd, Sunderland, Leicester, to name but six, the league was strong that season folks.

The League Cup was on us again and we drew Port Vale over two legs, quite a nice tie to start with and we saw them off 3-1 over two legs with Atkinson getting another couple of goals, he had started superbly in a Town shirt, me and Dad loved him he was so strong and energetic, just what we needed up front. We were on a bit of a roll or so we thought. The next five league games were a nightmare, we lost all five and only scored one goal, the wheels had certainly come off for those five games that was for sure everyone. We then went on a three game winning run, Orient were beaten 2-0 in the League Cup and we also won our next couple of league games but the season was very much up and down to say the least. Another couple of defeats in the league was really starting to get the crowd anxious and they were even worse when we were to go out of the League Cup 6-2 at Villa, Atkinson scoring again, omen for later on in his career who knows?? Although the season was very much up and down at least we were starting to see the emergence of some decent players in Atkinson, Lowe, Dozzell, Linighan, Kiwomya and especially Milton he was starting to really show why Ferguson brought him into the club from little Bury Town for £5,000, WHAT A BARGAIN!!

We would win only another two games out of the next six in the league, those being against Oldham and Leicester, we drew two and lost two, before we went to Forest in the FA Cup 3rd round, another quick exit, we lost 3-0 enough said no Wembley again this season! New Years had been and gone and in January it was to be the month we saw the first Russian to play in the football league his name Sergei Baltacha, what a signing he was, tall, elegant on the ball and he made his debut against Stoke at home on January 21st '89 and what a debut it turned out to be folks. We won 5-1 and totally outplayed the men from the Potteries with Dozzell netting twice, Kiwomya, Yallop and you guessed it Baltacha scoring for Town on his debut, Roy of the Rovers stuff you bet!!!

The next 15 league games were to finally decide our season, we won five, drew three and lost seven, too many if Ipswich Town were to get promotion. The season ended brilliantly with five wins out of five but too little too late I'm afraid everyone, another season in Division Two awaits I'm afraid, even worse, Dalian Atkinson was sold to Sheffield Wednesday and we hadn't even really seen the best of him, such a shame, I loved watching Dalian he was superb.

26 - WOULD JOHN DUCAN SURVIVE 1989-1990

After two eighth placed finishes in the Second Division something had to change at Ipswich Town I thought, or I could see the inevitable happening to John Duncan, now I certainly didn't dislike him as a person, and to a degree I didn't really dislike him as a manager, but wait a while was he getting results? No, and the pressure was on John Duncan to deliver that was for sure everyone. 1989-90 was to be the first season that I was to take my oldest son Ian to Portman Road, so now there were three generations of my family all going to games together, me, my dear father Eric and my son, although this season he only came to the odd game as at that time we weren't season ticket holders, it was easier because Ian was only six and I knew he wouldn't want to go every week, so we took him to the odd game or two and he loved it. Ian loved every sport going you see, especially football and cricket, he was to become an avid fan just like his Dad and Grandad were.

The season kicked off with Barnsley at home a good 3-1 win with Woods, Lowe and Humes scoring the goals, only 12,100 were in attendance a figure that was to be constant nearly all season apart from a 24,365 crowd at the West Ham Utd game, it is what it is as they say, things were much different back then, trust me everyone. We only won three out of the first twelve games and the season was always destined to be a bit of a struggle to get back to where we needed to be folks. David Lowe was a crowd favourite at the time and scored his fair share of goals but a new kid was coming to the fore in '89-'90 his name was Kiwomya soon to become a real favourite along with Dozzell etc. The League Cup didn't last long as we went out over the two legs to Tranmere 0-2 on aggregate, that League Cup eh!!

From October to New Years day we won eight games out of eleven, and drew the other three a remarkable run at the time and we were dreaming again, Kiwomya, Milton, Stockwell, Wark everyone was chipping in with goals at the time and I really started to believe again but wait! On New Years day I went with my mate up to Port Vale in the Potteries to watch us play, oh what a joke that game was, we lost 5-0 and it was a total embarrassment from start to finish, what an absolute shower of muck we were that day, but another ground ticked off as we true fans say!! I then travelled up to Leeds for an FA Cup tie at Elland Road, they were flying in the league, eventual champions, but we done a job on that lot and won 0-1 with Dozzell scoring, nearly as good a feeling as beating Norwich City for me, dirty Leeds and all that you see, from way back, people of my age know what I mean 100%.

In round four we were to come up against Barnsley at Oakwell, and it didn't go well, we were knocked out 2-0 and the season just went from bad to worse after that really. I said to Dad well we can concentrate on the league now and getting up, that went well didn't it.. NOT!! From the 14th January until the end of the season we played twenty two league games, winning eight, drawing five and losing nine, just not good enough and it eventually cost John Duncan his job, sad but inevitable I'm afraid everyone. He gave it his best shot I'm sure, but the job, too big for him, I have always maintained it was. Thank you John for what you did, but it just had to change, I think you knew that anyway. A ninth place finish again, just not good enough, the fanbase were getting restless to say the least, none more than me and my Dad, crowds were down, the football was dull and everything seemed like a chore when going to a match, it wasn't anything like I had known ever in my supporting life, EVER!!!

27 - WELCOME MR LYALL 1990-1991

Another dawn in Ipswich Town's history, Duncan had gone and the board appointed John Lyall a seasoned manager from West Ham Utd, a very good choice at the time I said to Dad, as he was so experienced, just what we needed to steady the ship as they say. He had a massive job on his hands, because like I've said before, confidence was low, fans were itching for success and attendances were at an all time low at the time, things had to change and quickly.

The season started with a home game against Sheffield Wednesday in front of 17,284 not a bad crowd at all but after a 0-2 defeat things were to unfortunately get worse as the attendances were as well. The first seven games were to bring three wins, one draw and three defeats, it was not one thing or the other really but everyone was more than happy to give Mr Lyall a chance, he was a top manager after all.

The League Cup was to pair us up against our good old friends from Shrewsbury, we always seemed to play them in the cups or that was what it felt like anyway, we beat them 4-1 over two legs and went through to play Southampton from Division One in the third round, a tie we lost 0-2 and out we went again, was I ever to see a League Cup final - 'PROBABLY NOT' was the answer one suggests.

The season like I said to Dad was okay, but we needed to kick on and get some wins and get up that table, how wrong I was, between September 29th and December 29th we played seventeen league games winning three, drawing ten, and losing four, seven of those draws were in a row, not promotion form at all I'm afraid everyone. Come the New Year we were miles off it and just seemed like another season in Division Two was inevitable, and so it was to be. The FA Cup was to be short lived a trip to play Southampton was not to be very fruitful and we got beat 3-2 with Dozzell getting both goals, a brave performance, but we went out at the 3rd round stage, something our younger supporters would get used to nearly every season a few years on unfortunately.

A New Year's day defeat at Oxford Utd, was followed by a decent set of results in the next nine games, we won five, drew two and lost only two but the season was already done really by now and we just hoped and prayed we would have a good run in to the end of the season and take it from there, but it was not to be, we struggled basically and we were glad really when it all came to an end. The last twelve games ARDUOUS at best and we won only two, drawing five and losing five, a sorry end to a sorry season that saw us finish fourteenth in the Second Division with 57 points a poultry total from what was a great football club.

John Lyall had the nucleus of a decent side on paper especially as he had already signed Goddard and Whitton would he be able to take Ipswich Town to the next level, time would tell as they say everyone, here's hoping.

28 - WHAT A SEASON THAT WAS
1991-1992

Well fellow Town fans, after a quite average season at best the previous season we were to be treated to an unbelievable season in '91-'92 that was for sure everyone. We had more or less the same squad apart from Gayle going to Sheffield Utd and Humes moving on to Wrexham, everything else was more or less the same, the only difference was everybody just clicked, not really a surprise because Lyall was such a good coach, and boy we were sure going to see it this season.

The season started off at Bristol Rovers, and what a start it was, we were coasting 0-3 up and then a certain young Marcus Stewart got involved and the game ended up 3-3, but we knew then that this was a different Town side although we had thrown it away, it was a team of skill, energy and had goals right through the team, most players chipping in. The next fifteen league games saw us win seven, draw six and lose only two, so a very good start to the season which we were to build upon later.

The League Cup was the only disaster we lost over two legs to Derby County 0-2, shame, but at least we could concentrate on the league 100% thank goodness everyone. The next three league games I remember vividly, the first two were at home against Sunderland (0-1) and that lot down the A14, Cambridge Utd. Now Cambridge were never really known as a footballing city, more for the colleges and rowing really, but at the time they had a decent side with the likes of Dublin and Claridge in their side. Anyway they came down to Portman Road and beat us 1-2 with Stockwell getting our goal, a shocking result for us really, but worse was to come because we lost our next game as well against Derby (A) 1-0 so no points out of nine and work to be done lads and Mr Lyall I may add.

I like everyone was loving the football we were playing and everybody was falling in love with the club again, the crowds still were not fantastic but who cared, I certainly didn't. I went to

Molineux to watch us play Wolves and we were back to winning ways with a great 1-2 win with Linighan and Dozzell getting the goals, only 11,915 at Wolves that day, oh how things have changed over the years everyone. After Molineux we played three games leading up to Christmas, we beat Tranmere (H) 4-0, lost at lowly Plymouth Argyle 1-0 and drew away at Swindon Town, who to be honest were a more than decent side at the time everyone.

Boxing day was upon us and we had Charlton at home and we duly beat them 2-0 with Kiwomya netting twice, believe it or not we were at home again two days later against the big spending Blackburn Rovers, 17,657 turned up for this game, and we played brilliantly to win the game 2-1 and send everybody home happy after what had been a superb Christmas, it was to get better on New Year's day as we played Port Vale again on that day, but this time winning 1-2 with Kiwomya again scoring twice, it was a great away day especially after losing there 5-0 two seasons ago.

The FA Cup was upon us again and we drew Hartlepool Utd, "good omen" I said to Dad, remember we played them the year we won the FA Cup everyone!! Well the game was not like 1978, we drew 1-1 at home (Dozzell) so we had to go all the way up to the North East for the replay, fortunately, we got the job done up there with Dozzell again and Milton putting us through, to set up a tie with Bournemouth at home in round four. We had three league games before we were to play Bournemouth, one defeat and two victories were claimed so we went to the cup tie in great heart indeed, we were playing some brilliant football at times, so pleasing on the eye. Bournemouth arrived at Portman Road not really expecting to go away with anything I would suggest and that is exactly how it turned out, they got beat 3-0 by Town at a canter, which set up a fantastic tie with high flying First Division Liverpool, a tie that will always live in the memory, more about that later everyone.

Town were on fire at this stage of the season, and three league wins on the trot against Bristol Rovers, Millwall and Portsmouth were to set us up nicely for the forthcoming home fifth round FA Cup tie with the scousers. The tie was on television but who wants to stay at home and watch on TV when Liverpool are in Town? No-one I hear you say, certainly not me, my dad, or Ian, it was so windy that day it really spoilt the game if I'm being honest, it really did, it was a scrappy game between two very good sides, and probably had a draw written all over it, and so it was, it finished 0-0 in front of 26,104 supporters, our best gate of the season for now! We played one game before we went to Anfield, a match at Penton Park against Tranmere, my first visit to Tranmere I may add, we won 0-1 with dear old Simon Milton getting the winner, these kind of results win you promotions let me tell you, 100% everyone. I stayed in Suffolk to watch the game at Liverpool, I watched it with my friends at The Pot Black club in Bury St Edmunds in front of the big screen, Dad came down as well, we had a few pints, jobs a good 'un as they say everyone!! Town played marvellous on the night and when Johnson scored in front of the bank of Town fans behind the goal at the Anfield Road end everyone went mental, beer everywhere, of course as everyone knows the game went to extra time and when Dozzell put us in front, we dared to dream for a while. The game was finally decided by what can only be described as moving the ball for a free kick to where Liverpool actually wanted to take it from and they duly scored, it was to be a tarnished finish to an absorbing cup tie, we lost 3-2 but how everyone, we had proved to everyone on live TV we were back!

The next four league games leading up to the game versus Cambridge Utd saw us win two, draw one and lose one so we were still in decent form. Now Cambridge away is never easy, even bearing in mind we normally have the lions share of the support and this game was no different. I like most went early and had a few beers, like you do, but the game itself was a typical Cambridge versus Ipswich game, it's always 100mph, tough tackling and all that, so I suppose we had to be thankful for a point, 1-1, with Milton scoring again. The next five games were pivotal in our quest for the title, Derby and Barnsley were both beaten, a great win against Derby who eventually finished third in the table, Dozzell scoring twice.We then went to Southend, who will forget Southend Utd away, I certainly won't. 10,003 packed into Roots Hall and a terrific atmosphere with thousands of Town fans in attendance. We won 1-2 with goals from Whelan and Thompson, Whelan having got into the side scored and Thompson hit a worldie into the top corner, everyone went ballistic, it was mental up our end behind the goal.

After the Southend game attendances got better and everyone was believing and quite rightly so. We had five games before the Oxford away game of which we won two, lost two and drew at home to Grimsby 0-0 in front of 22,393 fans, much much better indeed. So off we went to Oxford Utd at the old Manor Ground, a tiny little ground of such a funny shape as well to try and secure the title. It was a funny old game, a bitty, edgy affair if you like, a lot was at stake you see everyone. Me and Dad had gone on the coach to Oxford Utd, it was to seem like a lifetime during that game, Magilton scored for Oxford and Gavin Johnson scored for Ipswich, we drew 1-1, but that is all we needed to secure the title, brilliant scenes, we all including my Dad went on to the Oxford Utd pitch, celebrating widely, singing songs and dancing about. Ipswich kind of celebrated but it was difficult with all the fans on the pitch, so eventually home we went on the coach feeling ten feet tall, we were back, not only that we were to be part of the first ever Premier League - SUPERB!!

The last game of the season was against Brighton at home, 26,803 turned out on a lovely sunny day at Portman Road to see Mr Lyall receive the manager of the year award and also see the players receive the trophy and medals, everything was so relaxed, mainly because the job was already done at Oxford you see. We won the game 3-1 with Whitton 2, and Johnson scoring the last two goals of our magnificent season, thank you lads you were totally amazing all season long.

We had the traditional open top bus parade where thousands as usual turned out to celebrate what could only be described as brilliant, totally brilliant, every player gave everything, you cannot ask for more can you anyone? From a fourteenth place the previous season to a CHAMPIONSHIP winning season is unbelievable, thank you Mr John Lyall, thank you from myself, my dad and my sons, and every Town fan.

Premier League here we come as they say.

29 - BACK WHERE WE BELONG
1992-1993

After what can only be described as a wonderful season John Lyall took us into the inaugural season of the Premier League, what an honour for the club that was everyone. Aston Villa were the visitors on day one and with the stadium, one of the first to go all seated, it only had a capacity of about just over 22,000 and 16,818 were there for the first game. Gavin Johnson scored our first Premier League goal in a 1-1 draw that was to become a fantastic first season back in the top flight everyone.

The next ten games were to only bring one defeat against Oldham Athletic of all teams 4-2, the other nine producing amazingly six draws and three wins, two of which were against Wimbledon and the other against the reigning champions of the Football League Leeds United. Now if there was a team that me and Dad loved beating it was Leeds Utd, and on this particular day it was a magnificent game between two sets of champions from the previous season, it was an end to end game which flowed brilliantly, Town coming out on top 4-2 with goals from Wark (2), Kiwomya and Dozzell, a fantastic way to start your season off.

The League Cup had already started and we drew lowly Wigan in the second round and had no problem at all knocking them out 6-2 over the two legs, Portsmouth were up next in round three away and again a Thompson goal was enough to see us through 0-1 at their ground Fratton Park. The next league game in the Premier League was versus Chelsea a nice trip down to London, we lost 2-1 in front of a paltry crowd of 16,072 at Stamford Bridge, the next five league games were to produce three draws and two wins so we had got off to more than a decent start in our first season back in the Premier League, this was to help us no end come the end of the season everyone. The League Cup was back on our minds and we got a more than useful 2-2 draw at Villa, before beating them 1-0 at Portman Road, round five here we come! Me, Dad and Ian were really enjoying the season sitting in our seats in the North Stand, Yes, North Stand everyone never kept standing up all the time back then you see! We were unbeaten again in the next five league games up until Christmas and that included a fantastic 0-2 win at Carrow Road, Norwich, a game that was shown live on Sky TV, Kiwomya and Thompson securing the three points for the Town on the night, the Town fans went mental as usual when defeating Norwich, we also beat Blackburn on December 28th which again was a great win against one of the superpowers as they were known then under Jack Walker, Genchev and Kiwomya again seeing us home for three points.

The FA Cup was coming around once more and we were to draw Plymouth at home a game we won 3-1 with goals from Thompson, Dozzell and Whitton, a crowd of only 12,803 witnessed an easy win, to set up a tie with Tranmere away. Our league form had been decent but I remember thinking we need to push on just a little bit more, unfortunately we did the reverse and didn't pick up any points at all before the cup tie with Tranmere, we went there as the Premier League team and got the result we needed a 1-2 win with Dozzell and Genchev securing the victory a well earned win at a tough place to go. We had already played the 5th round tie against Sheffield Wednesday at home in the League Cup and a Whitton (pen) in front of 19,374 was enough to earn a replay at Hillsborough which we lost 1-0, that League Cup will haunt us forever more everyone. The FA Cup draw was always my favourite, listening to hear who we had got on the radio, and this time it was to be Grimsby Town at home, an ideal draw, that's exactly what I said to my Ian and Dad. Boncho was on fire that day, he scored a hat trick and I can still hear the North Stand singing "Boncho Boncho Boncho Boncho Boncho Boncho Boncho Genchev" great songs, great times everyone, by the way Warky got the other and we sailed through 4-0 without any trouble at all.

Me and Dad went to Spurs to watch in the Premier League, we won 0-2 and Yallop got a stormer, Genchev also scored and our fans went wild at White Hart Lane, literally. Believe it or not we followed that up with another win over Man Utd, Yallop scoring (AGAIN) and Kiwomya sealing the points over the future champions of the first Premier League, heady days indeed everyone. The next five league games were points wise, poor, we only picked up two points out of fifteen, two draws and three defeats, not good, but like I said a good job we had a solid start as me and Dad said loads of times together. We were in the last eight of the FA Cup again and we had a certain club called Arsenal coming to Town, we all remember playing that lot in the cup before, don't we everyone. It was televised on Match of the Day and what a game it was, it was on a knife edge at one stage, but the gunners ran out 2-4 winners in the end, with Kiwomya and Genchev scoring for the Town. No Wembley final this time folks.

The last eleven games of the league season saw us win two, draw two and lose seven, thank god for that start everyone. The two wins were special, I know beating Norwich was fantastic, especially doing the double over them by winning 3-1, but for me the best match was versus Forest, we won 2-1, but it was Brian Clough's last ever match, we gave him a standing ovation, when he came out, and he gave James Scowcroft a kiss, typical Cloughie, his son Nigel Clough scored their goal, a fitting end to quite a brilliant career, farewell Brian x.

30 - ANOTHER LEGEND DEPARTS THE CLUB 1993-1994

With finances still not brilliant another absolute legend was to leave our football club, Jason Dozzell who had given ten marvellous seasons to the club was on his way to White Hart Lane, the players we brought in were to be Marshall, Mason and Slater from Celtic. Unbelievably Marshall was to make his debut at Oldham Athletic the club he had just left to join Town. I thought I must see this so I went up to Oldham for my very first visit to the ground, I wasn't disappointed as we won 0-3 and Marshall scored one of the goals along with Steve Palmer and Paul Mason, a fine start to any season I thought.

We won the next two games against Southampton (1-0) and Chelsea (1-0) with Marshall getting both goals, he was an instant North Stand hero, nine points out of nine, we were top of the table, well we were for a while! We played Norwich away next, I said to Dad we are playing them just at the right time, we were on a lovely winning run, how wrong was I, we lost 1-0 and that started a rather drab run for us unfortunately. The next seven league games produced only four points out of twenty one, we didn't win a game, four draws and three defeats, not Premier League staying up for that and we all knew it. In between we had played another cup tie with Cambridge Utd, this time over two legs we actually won for a change 4-1 on aggregate, happy days for once, especially at the Abbey Stadium, it was just so nice to go there and win for a change, so nice! We won at Wimbledon 0-2, a very good win at the time as they were very hard to beat at the time, especially at home. The League Cup third round was next and we were at Liverpool at Anfield, we put on a decent performance before bowing out 3-2, Marshall and Mason with the goals for Town, that League Cup eh!

We had eight league games up to when we played Norwich just before Christmas on the 18th December, we won two, drew four and lost two before that infamous game against the canaries at Portman Road. Now Derby Day is Derby Day but when you get a penalty award to you and you have Wark in the side you are laughing even more so if the visitors score an own goal even better. We went in front after 8 minutes, with Wark converting a penalty, Bowen equalised only for Megson to score a 90th minute own goal, you couldn't write it, it was brilliant, the crowd went wild. A draw against West Ham at home and a defeat to Liverpool both at Portman Road was to set the tone for a very tough second half of the season. We drew Swindon Town away at the County Ground in the FA Cup, we drew 1-1 with Ian Marshall scoring to set up a replay at Portman Road, the replay went to extra time, but Town squeezed through 2-1 to set up a great cup tie with Spurs at home. Our next two league games were to be 0-0 draws before we played Spurs in the fourth round of the FA Cup, we played super football against Tottenham and went through 3-0 quite easily I may add. The next three league games brought only one point out of nine, we really were starting to get in quite a bit of trouble if we didn't start winning a few, 100%. Wolves away was next in the cup a game we could win and after a good result 1-1 at Molineux with a goal from Wark, we all felt pretty confident coming home from the game about the replay, we lost 1-2 at home in the replay with Palmer notching our goal, no Wembley this season!

We had to start winning a few games and we did manage a couple, Sheffield Utd was massive and we won 3-2 in a game we could not afford to lose, thanks to Linighan, Marshall and Slater we saw them off. The next vital win came at Villa Park. It was a superb win 0-1, with Johnson getting the winner, oh how we enjoyed that win especially against them!! It was oh so vital because in the last eleven league games we won one, drew four and lost seven a disastrous run only saved on the last day at Blackburn, we got a hard earned point at runners up elect Blackburn and Sheffield Utd were losing at Chelsea a result that sent them down and kept Ipswich Town in the PREMIER LEAGUE for now anyway. 19th place in the league should have been a wake up call, was it, you tell me everyone!

31 - TOTAL HUMILIATION 1994-1995

Season 1993-94 was a struggle from start to finish and this season was to prove probably the worst I and my family had witnessed to date, it was at times very hard to watch, indeed at times you really wanted to be hiding behind your sofa. Players kept coming and going and during the season we added Chapman, Mathie, Sedgley and Thomsen. Taricco and Swailes came in later, Gregory, Genchev, Johnson, Kiwomya and Youds went out, it was time for change again folks.

After saying goodbye to Mr Clough a couple of season ago we started our season at home toa very good Forest side, we lost 0-1 and that was very much to set the tone for what was to become arguably one of the clubs worst ever seasons in the Football League, certainly the worst in my lifetime that was for sure. Andrew was going with me, Dad and Ian by this stage, but as a very young lad he didn't care, he just was pleased to be watching top flight football at his favourite club, bless him. After drawing 1-1 at Wimbledon, a decent result with Milton scoring the goal, me and Dad went on the coach to QPR, now there's hot days and there are scorching days and this was one of those, it was roasting, god knows where the players got their energy from on that day to be honest with you. They rallied and we won the game 1-2 and afterwards me and Dad were desperate to find a shop that sold cold water, we found one and it was heaven, trust me everyone. By the time we played that lot from down the A140 in the derby, we had been very much up and down with results and it was no different when we played Norwich City a 1-2 defeat at home with Wark (pen) the only consolation on a totally crap day, it was always a crap day losing to that lot. We had a League Cup tie against Bolton over two legs of which we lost 0-4 on aggregate, a terrible couple of results against a lower league side. In between the games with Bolton we had a massive game on our hands with Man Utd at home and what a game it turned out, Utd had obviously all their superstars, Beckham, Scholes etc. but we on the night had HEART and that counted for a lot, we managed to win 3-2 in an epic match with Mason scoring two and Segley getting the other, a magical performance on a night just after we had lost to Norwich, a superb effort by everyone, it was a result that was to HAUNT us later on in the season, more about that later everyone.

By this time of the season early October, we were out of the League Cup (AGAIN), and our results were indifferent to say the least but we had to somehow believe. After the Man Utd game we played thirteen games in the League and only came away victorious once and that was against Leeds Utd at home thanks to Sedgley and Williams, we won 2-1 but the writing was most certainly already on the wall. The other twelve games produced three draws and nine (9) defeats, something had to change and change it did, Mr George Burley was back, thank goodness, one of my idols of the '70s and '80s was back, I loved it and so did my family especially my Dad. We had just got a useful draw at West Ham on Boxing Day 1-1- so George Burley came into the game against Arsenal with at least a tiny piece of hope, and my it was tiny everyone, results were not good, confidence was low and the fans by and large feared the worst.

Anyway to Burleys first game versus Arsenal, I can see him walking down that touchline now with his Ipswich coat on that always seemed two sizes too big for him, bless him, but joking aside it was so brilliant to see an Ipswich Town man back at the helm, especially George who for years had been brought up by Bobby Robson, say no more folks! The game itself didn't go very well really and we lost 0-2 to Arsenal but it was so great just to see Burley back it really was everyone. Everton away was next up for George but again like I said before confidence was through the floor and we got soundly beat 4-1, where to now? Well everything was so hard to predict at the time a New Years game against Leicester City saw us play particularly well and we carved City apart to beat them 4-1 with Kiwomya scoring two, Tanner and Yallop getting the others, this was to prove to be Kiwomyas last goals for the Town before signing for Arsenal.

Next up was the FA Cup one of me and Dads favourite days of the season, we drew Wrexham at the Racecourse ground, brilliant I said to Dad we haven't been there which was true, neither of us had been to Wrexham so another one to tick off, do I wish I stayed at home? Not really everyone. There were only 8,324 in attendance but at times, and especially when they scored it seemed like 28,000 were there, but we got what we deserved, nothing, we lost 2-1 with Linighan scoring our goal. It was humiliation, but not as bad as what was to come later in the season, everyone. The next Saturday we were at Anfield, now with no disrespect I and loads of other fans had seen Town mauled on occasions at Anfield with by FAR better players than we had in 1995, we had nowhere near the team like we had in the 60's, 70's or 80's but guess what happened, we won, YES WON, with Adam Tanner scoring the winner. I, my Dad, my boys or anybody couldn't believe it, and especially with the season we were having, WELL DONE GEORGE bless you! We followed this up with a good draw against a lively Chelsea team 2-2 at Portman Road but we needed wins and we just were not getting enough of them unfortunately everyone. This season was starting to really run away from us and it wasn't helped by the next five results against Blackburn (A), Palace (H), Man City (A), Southampton (H) and Newcastle (H) we lost four out of the five, with the only win coming against Southampton 2-1, Chapman and Mathie scoring the goals, their first for the Town. This led to the biggest HUMILIATION I or any of my family, including my Dad, who had been going for longer than anyone in our family, had ever witnessed.

We all went on the coach to Old Trafford, there was me, my Dad, Ian and Andrew, and also on the coach was my brother John and his son Tristan, it was a real family day out to Lancashire. We arrived in decent time to have a good look around the ground and Ian and Andrew loved it, this was THE ground to visit, so much history to be found, Law, Best, Charlton and all that everyone. To the game itself, we were always under the cosh from the first whistle and in front of a crowd of 43,804 Keane opened the scoring before Andy Cole added two more before half time. In the second half United scored four times in the first twenty minutes to lead 7-0, Cole had scored another two and Hughes had also scored twice. Then Paul Ince scored United's eighth goal while Forrest was arguing with Graham Poll, a joke an absolute joke everyone, after the dust had settled Cole scored his fifth goal in a 9-0 win, this was a total humiliation, something I never ever want to witness EVER AGAIN THANK YOU, there was a time during the game when Town fans tongue in cheek were singing we want ten (10) they didn't really obviously, it was just one of those days, but please Town never again!! I remember going home thinking about the stick I was going to get from workmates etc. for months ahead but funnily enough I didn't get much due to the fact I actually started to think people were starting to feel sorry for us. I felt so sorry for George, as he was Town through and through but he like us had to brush himself down and just get on with it, good luck with that George!

Get on with it we did, well kind of everyone, we had eleven league games to play, and after the Old Trafford debacle, we only scored one goal in the next five league games and that was in a 0-1 defeat at home to QPR in front of 11,767 fans, awful days indeed everyone, in that run we even lost 3-0 at Norwich and they went down with us, say no more everyone. I must admit though even though they went down with Ipswich, they did finish 16 points above our total of points, embarrassing to say the least my dear friends. The last six games of the season saw us win one game, draw one and lose four, we went down with a whimper and it couldn't come soon enough for any of us, it was totally embarrassing. The last win we did have was against Coventry City, Marshall and a Pressley own goal in a 2-0 win being our last goals in the top flight until the next time, and with George Burley in charge we all thought it would only be a matter of time until the NEXT TIME.

Oh well we were relegated, but we needed to go down and rebuild, we just were not good enough for the Premier League FULL STOP EVERYONE. It was in this close season on July 6th 1995 my dear wife Venetia lost her father Joe, a lovely man who devoted his life to his family and also to his beloved football club Ipswich Town. He was a season ticket holder in the blue seats in the Cobbold Stand for years, and when he was not so well he used to give his two season tickets to myself and my dad to use, more often for night games when it was too cold for Joe to attend. He was a true blue, always and forever in our hearts, love you Joe, RIP - Colin, Venetia, Ian, Andrew, Jo, Ella, Maisie and Alice xxxxxxxx

32 - BACK INTO THE 2ND TIER
1995-1996

Mr Burley was certainly having a clear out at the club and Chapman, Linigham, Palmer, Slater and Neil Thompson were all to exit the club, he really was starting to build his own squad, and I for one was very excited by the prospect of him building for the future, after all he had worked under Mr Robson for a lot of years, I trusted him 100% everyone.

As a football supporter it's difficult to get your head round relegation, and especially after a season like we had just had, we only won seven games out of forty-two (as it was then) in the Premier League and it takes guts to fight back from that everyone. The season didn't start brilliant in the Second Tier, we had an opener at St. Andrews, Birmingham and we lost 3-1 but we had to believe we were good enough to at least make the play-offs, so heads up everyone.

The next seven games produced four wins, two draws and a single defeat, so not all bad, one of the wins was 3-0 at home to eventual champions Sunderland with Mathie getting a hat trick to boot. Mathie and Marshall were becoming a lethal partnership, me, Dad, and the boys loved a bit of M&M. That famous League Cup was upon us again the less said about it the better, we drew Stockport over two legs and lost 3-2 on aggregate, NOT GOOD EVERYONE, that League Cup I hear you say AGAIN! Things take time in football and George certainly needed time, the next nine games were to be honest not good, starting with a thumping at home by Charlton 1-5, it wasn't to get much better as we only won one game against Reading, we won one, drew three and lost five if you included the Charlton game, not good at all!! We had to get some results together and get them together we did, up until New Years day we played seven league games and won three, drew four, so points were being picked up on a more regular basis, and the play-offs could still be reached.

In the FA Cup we drew Blackburn and drew 0-0 at home only to go to Ewood Park in the replay and win 0-1, I went to that game and Wright had what could only be described as the game of his life, he saved everything, especially from Shearer, Shearer I can still see him now with his head in his hands, he couldn't believe how good Wright was, he was sensational on the night, a great, great win. We played Walsall in the next round and won 1-0 with Mason scoring again, he had got the winner at Blackburn as well by the way, so it was to be another Premier League team Aston Villa in the fifth round at home and although Mason notched once more we got beat 1-3 and Wembley was over again for another year.

The league form since January was decent, a few defeats but generally form was okay. In the sixteen games since New Year leading up to the Norwich City game we won eight, drew two and lost six, it was that kind of season, okay, but not okay if you know what I mean everyone! Anyway it was Derby Day again and Norwich who were having an average season at best came to Portman Road, the atmosphere, although neither side were pulling up trees, was still electric, it always is as any Town or City fan will tell you, it is the best Derby to play in for most people. Ian Marshall scored for Ipswich and then later in the game the most outrageous own goal you will ever see by Ullathorne up the Churchmans end sent everyone delirious, it was great, superb, fantastic and also very, very funny, we won 2-1 and it will go down in East Anglian Derby match history. After that we went to lowly Tranmere and got beat 5-2, also lovely Southend and lost 1-2, although we won two and drew one of our last three games, it was to be Second Tier football for us again in 1996-97, sad but it is what it is, Tony Mowbray signed for us late in the '95-'96 season, what a signing he was to turn out to be for us everyone.

33 - PLAY OFFS PLEASE GEORGE 1996-1997

The previous season had been alright, but we needed to kick on this season, we had good hungry young players coming through like Scowcroft, Naylor etc. to add to the players of senior experience we already had, it looked good indeed. Thomsen was sold to Everton and Marshall was to go to Leicester, no worries, George knew what he was doing don't worry. By this time we were all sitting in the Pioneer Lower family enclosure, I say Pioneer because I am old school and will never change, the boys loved it down there because they were closest to the action, always good when you are young.

We lost at Man City on the opening day 1-0, not a very good start considering City were bang average at the time and eventually would finish 14th, Our first home game was Reading and we hammered them 5-2 but the crowds were still awful with only 9,767 in attendance everything about the club needed a pick me up and like I kept saying to Dad, George was the man to do it, I was convinced he was. The first ten games we were starting to get it right to a certain degree, we won three, drew five and lost two, steady but we were getting there everyone. The League Cup was upon us and we drew Bournemouth over two legs winning 5-1 and so we got to play Fulham again over two legs and put them to the sword 5-3 on aggregate. Next up was the local derby at Norwich, now I come from an era of not losing many times at all to that lot so to start losing to them came very hard to myself, this time we got beat 3-1 with Sonner scoring our goal, enough said, another long 40 mile journey home well it seemed it anyway everyone. The League Cup draw had paired us with Palace in the 3rd Round and we turned it on again to go through 4-1 at home, we played the next round versus Gillingham in round four, four days later and beat them 1-0 to reach the fifth round where we would play Leicester in the New Year.

By this stage of the season and taking into account we were into the fifth round of the League Cup you would have been entitled to think crowds were on the up, but you would have been totally wrong, we were averaging about 11,500 at best it wasn't good at all everyone. Our next sixteen games up to New Year, we won five, drew five and lost six, very much up and down but we were still in the mix if we could pick it up after New Year, the FA Cup was short lived, we lost 3-0 at Forest and we didn't deserve anything out of the tie, trust me everyone. Jason Cundy had joined the club and what a difference he made, he was solid, read the game brilliantly and became a very good leader on the pitch. Cundy had scored his first goal for the club back in November at Bradford City and was to repeat it at Barnsley when we won 2-1, a game that was to set us on a great run of form in the league.

In the last eighteen games of the season we won eleven, drew four and lost only three, in that run we thrashed WBA 5-0, Oldham 4-0 and Swindon away 0-4, we always won at Swindon, a great away day that! We beat Norwich City 2-0 in the derby with Tarrico and Mason scoring in front of 22,397 that's more like it everyone a decent crowd!

Into the playoffs we went and played the canaries of the North, Sheffield United, we were away first and we drew 1-1, quite a good result I thought, WRONG! The second leg at Portman Road a game in which I think we all thought was a certain Town win, finished up a 2-2 draw with Scowcroft and Gudmundsson scoring the goals. Unfortunately at the time away goals counted double, so we went out on away goals cruel, very cruel but at least we were getting there, slowly but surely.

Andrew and Ian pictured with George Burley

34 - DEMOLITION DERBY 1997-1998

One of the clubs best signings in my opinion, was to come to the club this season it was Matt Holland, he was probably the best signing this club has made since Mariner, Muhren and Thijssen came to the club, also Petta was starting to come to the fore as was a certain Kieron Dyer what a player he was becoming out of the youth team.

We started the season with a trip to Loftus Road, how many times have we said that over the years everyone, anyway, we drew 0-0 but a points a point and we were on our way. We drew Charlton in the League Cup and beat them 4-1 over two legs, quite comfortably as well, the next round was against Torquay United over two legs, first leg at home which we drew 1-1 so all on the second leg at Torquay. Now I hadn't been to Torquay so I thought I must go to that game. I went on the Bury coach, we went early and we arrived in Torquay about lunchtime so we had all afternoon to ourselves, it was heaven on the beer all day, well at least until 6pm anyway, when the coach picked us up again and took us to Torquay, by this time we had had a few and everyone was in good spirits. We won the game easily 0-3 and we all had some of the nicest pasties you could ever want to eat. It was an amazing trip. I didn't get back to Angel Hill, Bury St Edmunds until about 4am, I was very tired, knackered, in fact so was everyone. The league form was sketchy to say the least and in the first seven games including QPR we only won once, drawing three and losing three which included another derby defeat at Norwich 2-1 with Stein scoring our only goal of the game. We won our next game at home to an awful Manchester City 1-0 with Mathie getting the winner, Man City were eventually to be relegated to the third tier of English football at the end of the season, HOW TIMES HAVE CHANGED EVERYONE.

The next game was to be Man Utd in the League Cup third round and what a game it turned out to be, yes Utd had made some changes but Town played out of their skins and duly won 2-0 with goals from Mathie and Tarrico, the ground went mental when Tarrico scored and quite rightly, the goal was a worldie into the top corner of the net. We were still finding it hard to get a run together in the league and our next eight games only produced one win against lowly Bury, we had four draws and three defeats of which one was against Stockport County at home 0-2 in front of 8,939 fans, which at the time was our lowest crowd at home for any league match. I remember saying to Dad how much lower can things get, if only I had a crystal ball I hear you say everyone.

The League Cup was back again and we drew Oxford away, a game we won 1-2 with Dozzell and Mowbray scoring in front of a paltry 5,723 home fans tinpot or what? At least it set up a mouth watering game with Chelsea in round five. Our form in the league was still up and down and in the next eight games leading up until Christmas we won four, drew two and only lost two, so not all bad leading up to the New Year. We drew Bristol Rovers again in the FA Cup and after a 1-1 draw down there we beat them 1-0 at home with Johnson netting the goal. In between we had an epic League Cup tie against Chelsea at Portman Road a game in which Tarrico and Mathie both scored again, it ended 2-2 (a.e.t) and it went to penalties. Chelsea showed their international class and won 4-1 on penalties, a super night though for everyone that night, it was cup ties all the way at the moment and we played our old foes Sheffield Utd in the fourth round of the FA Cup and after drawing the first game 1-1, we lost the replay 1-0 and went out.

That cup defeat was to prove a blessing because league form certainly improved after that and we went on a very good run of games leading up to the derby game we played seven games, winning four and drawing three, not bad form going into a massive match with your arch rivals Norwich. This derby game was like no other really, we attacked the Churchmans end first half and before you knew it we were one-nil up thanks to Alex Mathie, we were on fire and Norwich had no answer to our skill and pace, Mathie helped himself to another two goals before half time and with the match ball to boot, he also injured himself so didn't come out for the second half. No matter Ipswich Town were not to be denied and they just kept doing what all Burley sides did, attack. Now we've seen some City sides over the years out on their backsides but this Norwich City side were completely done for, they didn't know what had hit them and another two goals were put away by Bobby Petta and the DEMOLITION DERBY was complete, two words to the players and George Burley "THANK YOU". We now had a run in that really didn't look too bad on paper and out of the last fourteen games we won eleven, drew two and only lost once and that was to the eventual champions Nottingham Forest, in that run I went to my first ever game at Stockport, a game which Mr Sheepshanks gave me a ticket to go in because I was soaking wet in the rain outside the ground.

We bombed into the playoffs finishing fifth in the table only to lose to Charlton 2-0 over two legs, a very disappointing end to a very good season everyone.

35 - AN END OF AN ERA 1998-1999

This season in particular will ALWAYS go down in my memory as one of the saddest in my life and also my boys lives as it was as they say an END OF AN ERA, more of that later everyone. George was starting to really build something by this time and players were coming and going until he got what he thought was an Ipswich Town team playing the IPSWICH WAY, it was taking a bit of time but slowly it was starting to come. Dyer was becoming a major influence in midfield and with players like Holland, Mowbray, Wright and Venus in the side the future looked bright, VERY BRIGHT everyone and with Magilton and Wilnis to join later on it looked very good indeed.

The season started with a trip to Grimsby, now Grimsby is not the best place to go in the world at anytime really, but in August is probably the best time, the ground is right beside the coast only a short walk from the beach and on this day it was lovely and warm, after witnessing the game itself which ended 0-0 we probably would have been better off doing a bit of sunbathing on the beach everyone. The next trip was another long one down to Exeter in the League Cup, it was a long trip but worth it because I had to get it knocked off my long list of away grounds, I sat in the side stand there and we drew 1-1, we won the second leg so went through comfortably in the end, we played Luton in the second round and lost 5-4 on aggregate, out again but by no means the end of the world folks!! We were finding scoring goals difficult in the first four games, in fact the first three games ended 0-0 but we weren't getting beaten which was a plus. The next fifteen league games up until around about bonfire night we won ten, drew two and lost only three, one of those being at home to that lot down the A140 0-1 but we won't dwell on that everyone.

It was around this time of the season when my dad was not very well at all, and he had an appointment at the West Suffolk hospital in Bury St. Edmunds and it was diagnosed that he had stomach cancer. He was so brave during the next few months, tired, weak, all of those things, but we still did what we could to make the best of a very bad time. I wrote to the club and met up with Holland,

Cundy, Wright and Johnson, we had a tour of the ground, changing rooms, etc, it was lovely, we even had a meal in the Centre Spot restaurant with the players. Dad had his photograph taken on the pitch in the goal up the Churchmans end, something I know he treasured immensely everyone. By February time dad was so sill he couldn't really do much at all and eventually he was to go to St. Nicholas hospice where he spent the last days of his life, he was so brave in there even one of the nurses said to me one day I went to visit, and your dad was on his hands and knees trying to get to the toilet so he didn't have to disturb us, that was my Dad a true gentleman, my hero, my friend, my fellow football fan. I miss him as much today as I ever have done, we did so much together, we travelled the length and breadth of the country and also Europe together "DAD I LOVE YOU". He died on March 8th 1999, god bless him and after the funeral I decided I must do something to remember Dad forever at our favourite place, Portman Road. So I found a piece of Dads oak in his shed and got a piece of brass and had a plaque made for me in memory of my father, when made it looked lovely, I showed it to David Sheepshanks and the board they allowed me to have it put up on the brick work of the Pioneer stand very near to where Dad last sat with his last season ticket. Alan Ferguson put it up for me and I clean it all the time, so it always looks lovely, great memories indeed, of a super Ipswich Town fan and Dad xxxxx.

During dad's illness obviously the season went on and it was difficult for me because my mind was all over the place at the time, thinking of dad, but we continued to go along at a very good rate of knots.

In the seven games leading up until Christmas, we won four, drew one and lost two, so still in decent promotion form really. New Year was on us and I decided to go to Tranmere for the FA Cup and we won 1-0 and guess who scored the goal, McGreal (own goal) you couldn't write it could you, MrGreal who was to become a Town Legend the very next season. We lost a couple of games on the trot before we played Everton away in the FA Cup a game we lost

1-0 but it meant we could 100% concentrate on the league which was good.

Sunderland were ripping it up in our league and were proving too much to stay with, but Bradford were very much in our sights most of the time. From the FA Cup tie we played eighteen games until the end of the season and we won twelve, drew two and lost four, one of which was the day after I lost my father a 3-2 defeat at Palace, a game I so wanted to win for obvious reasons everyone. Norwich away was a boring 0-0 draw in front of 19,511, yes 19,511 they haven't always had 28,000 you younger Ipswich fans take note. So it was play offs again and it was to be sixth place Bolton.

We went to Bolton and got beat 1-0, not a tragic result under the circumstances and we always thought going into the second leg it was ours for the taking, WRONG!! As usual it was an unbelievable game against Bolton and we won 4 3 on the night with Holland (2) and Dyer (2) scoring the goals, who will forget Kieron Dyer at the end after we had lost on away goals, absolutely devastated as we all were, Dyer, Mathie, Sonner and Tarrico were to leave the club and another rebuilding of the team was to start, for the good, who knows!? We will see. A disappointing end to an awful year for myself and my family, it could only get better surely everyone!

On the 28th April 1999 Ipswich Town lost the great Sir Alf Ramsey, he was the Ipswich manager that won the 1st Division title in 1962 and then famously went on to win the World Cup with England in 1966, a fantastic man and manager. Sir Alf R.I.P.

Colin, Jason Cundy and Dad Eric

RIP – Sir Alf Ramsey

Diary of an Obsession

RIP – Eric Plumb – pictured here on his 70th birthday in his Royal Marine Blazer at the Rushbrooke Arms, Sicklesmere

A memory for Eric Plumb which can be seen in the West Stand –
behind entrance to Block JJ (tap it for good luck!)

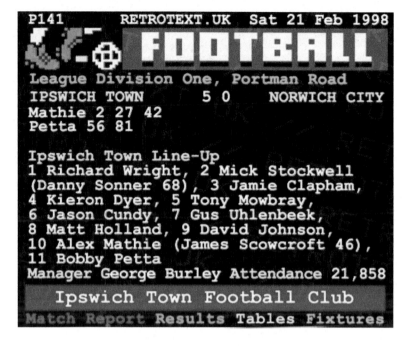

FOOTBALL

League Division One, Portman Road
IPSWICH TOWN   5 0   NORWICH CITY
Mathie 2 27 42
Petta 56 81

Ipswich Town Line-Up
1 Richard Wright, 2 Mick Stockwell
(Danny Sonner 68), 3 Jamie Clapham,
4 Kieron Dyer, 5 Tony Mowbray,
6 Jason Cundy, 7 Gus Uhlenbeek,
8 Matt Holland, 9 David Johnson,
10 Alex Mathie (James Scowcroft 46),
11 Bobby Petta
Manager George Burley Attendance 21,858

Ipswich Town Football Club
Match Report Results Tables Fixtures

Teletext shows the final score in the Demolition Derby

36 - REUSER PREMIERSHIP
1999-2000

1999-00 was the first season since 1964-65 that I was to go to Portman Road without my dad, it was not a very nice feeling at all, but at least I still had my two boys Ian and Andrew to go with so it was not all bad as they say everyone. After such a great season the season before, could we go the extra mile and gain promotion? Me and the boys were still sitting in the family enclosure at the bottom of the Pioneer stand, but like I said it wasn't the same without Dad banging on the advertising boards at the back of the stand. Attendances were a lot better by now, what with our superb end to the previous season, we opened up with Forest at home and we won 3-1 with Naylor, Johnson and Scowcroft scoring the goals in front of 20,830 very happy Town fans, was this the start of something brilliant, who knows?

George had changed things again a little in the summer with McGreal coming in to play alongside Mowbray and later on he was to bring in Croft, Wright, Reuser and of course a certain Marcus Stewart, what a signing he was. The League Cup came and went as usual we drew Brentford over two legs and we won 4-0, only to play Crewe in round two and get beat 3-2 on aggregate, a blessing in disguise we might all say everyone. I watched the Swindon game in August on Sky Sports and we thumped them 1-4 at the County Ground, my god we played well, we were on the warpath that was for sure. The next nine games produced four wins, two draws and three defeats, not too bad at all, we were certainly playing some excellent football and the crowds were decent. I went to Walsall. I hadn't been there before so another ground ticked off my list, it's a weird little ground situated right next to the motorway. Tiny little stand we were in but as usual the Town fans made the atmosphere and we came away with a 0-1 win with Naylor notching the winner in front of a paltry 6,526 supporters.

We lost the next game to eventual runners up Man City at Maine Road 1-0 another game I went to in front of 32,799 a proper crowd in a proper old stadium, walking through Moss side after the game isn't always a nice experience but they had won so it wasn't too bad. The next twelve games leading up to New Year were brilliant, we were on a great run of form and we managed to win six, we drew five and lost only one to Huddersfield 3-1, the club that would eventually sell us Stewart, thank you very much Mr Bruce. Again in the FA Cup we drew Southampton and I and the boys lost no sleep at all at losing to them 0-1, it was the best thing that could have happened to us. Over the next four games in the league we won two and drew two leading up to a game we had at Barnsley that I shall never forget, we had travelled up to Oakwell to see the game and what a game! Barnsley were going well in the league but so were we and we won the game 0-2 with Scowcroft and a magnificent goal from Stewart giving us the points, we had loads at the ground behind the goal going mental, promotion who knows? After the Barnsley game we had sixteen games to go in the season and we won nine, drew three and lost four which left us two points behind Man City which meant another season in the play offs, which would match us up with our old friends from Bolton Wanderers AGAIN!! Because we finished third that meant we were at the Reebok Stadium first, which in my mind was a good thing, well I thought that at first I'd probably started changing my mind when we were 2-0 down but hey ho! It was only then when we were 2-0 down that a certain Marcus Stewart really came to the party and how!! He scored an absolute beauty into the top corner to make it 2-1 just before half time and then later scored what can only be described as a WORLDIE finish dancing past the Bolton keeper and smacking it in the net for 2-2, he like all the Town fans went ballistic, it was game on everyone.

The Bolton home game will always live in the memory as one of the most unbelievable games in the history of Portman Road football. It all started off by Holdsworth giving Bolton the lead by bundling in the six yard box 0-1, then we got a penalty that Magilton scored and it was all up in the air again until Holdsworth again scored with a free kick that me and my boys were directly behind it was in all the way 1-2. We then missed a penalty before half time again it was Magilton but unfortunately this time the keeper saved it, 1-2 at half time. The second half started with a bang and super Jim Magilton then made it 2-2 with a fine finish up the North Stand end, only for Bolton to go straight up the other end and score again through Alan Johnston a super goal, 2-3, Wright then made a brilliant save from Jensen to keep it at 2-3 thank goodness everyone. The game was still on a knife edge and who should turn up and get the equaliser right near the end, yes you've guessed it Magilton scored again to complete his hat trick 3-3, the crowd were going mental at this stage, but that was not the end of it before the end of normal time because Bolton had Whitlow sent off just before Knight was to end normal time Bolton were down to ten men, game on everyone!! Extra time started and Town were well on top by this time and it was only a matter of time before we scored and we did in the first half of extra time when Clapham scored another penalty after one of our players was hauled to the ground, we were 4-3 up for the first time we had been winning in the whole tie, let alone the second leg everyone. There was still time for another Bolton player Elliott to be sent off, mistiming a challenge over by the Cobbold stand, they were down to nine men and had totally lost the plot. But we kept going forward just like all Burley sides did and we finally put the last nail in Boltons coffin thanks to a delightful finish by Mr Reuser 5-3, 7-5 on aggregate. Was that to be an OMEN who knows everyone, WHO KNOWS? Burley had finally made it to Wembley and who could say he or the players didn't deserve it after the previous seasons of play off disappointment, no one! GOOD LUCK TOWN!

It was now off to Wembley for the final and on a lovely sunny day as it normally is for Wembley finals my wife Venetia also came along with me and the boys, she enjoys a big day out does Venetia. We had seats on the side at Wembley quite a few rows back and a marvellous view. The game started off with both teams feeling each other out, but it was Barnsley who scored first a screamer by Hignett hits the bar rebounds off Wright and into the net 0-1 not a good start, it gets even worse in the 20th minute because Johnson has to go off with an injury sustained early in the match and Naylor replaces him. Ipswich were really starting to put the pressure on by this stage and we equalised from a Magilton corner which Mowbray powered into the top corner with a header

1-1, the crowd went wild. Ipswich were all over Barnsley at this stage but you wouldn't believe it Barnsley got forward and Wright brought Hignett down a penalty was given and Barnard has it saved by Wright to his right, thank you Wrighty you have saved the day big man!!

The second half is quite even for the first little while and then Ipswich burst into life, a long ball is flicked on by Stewart and straight into Naylors path, he waits for Miller to come before deftly flicking past him from 15 yards out, a magnificent finish, it's shirt off time Mr Naylor 2-1 Town, after 51 minutes. It really was all Town by this stage and we duly went 3-1 ahead in the 57th minute when a great touch by Naylor released Clapham out wide and he delivered the ultimate cross for Stewart who headed into the corner, a truly brilliant goal and build up. It was end to end at this point and both sides had great chances to score but both sides squandered their chances of scoring. Hristov had come on for Barnsley and was causing quite a few problems for the Town defence, he was big and strong and I couldn't quite make out why he didn't start to be fair. Naylor nearly made it 4-1 when he was clear but put his shot into Millers Arms. After 77 minutes Barnsley did get a goal back and it was another penalty, Thomas was brought down by Mowbray and Hignett made no mistakes, 3-2 and it was getting very edgy indeed especially when Hristov had a point blank header to make it 3-3 but fortunately Wright saved it and it remained 3-2 to Ipswich. By this time George had brought on Reuser and what an impact he was to bring to the party. Barnsley were going for it big time as you would in their position but then the final nail in Barnsley's coffin, the ball was with Naylor on the half way line and he somehow managed to get it back to Reuser, he went on a diagonal run towards the Barnsley goal and when he got to the edge of the box he just unleashed an unstoppable cross shot and as the commentator said it's

REUSER PREMIERSHIP

Music to all our ears everyone.

Oh my goodness how lovely it was to hear that final whistle everyone was so, so happy George, Dale, players, David Sheepshanks and most importantly us lot the fans, my god had we been through it in the last three years, we had been to hell and back that was for sure everyone. Ipswich went up and Holland lifted that lovely silver trophy up, we were back where I and everyone knows we deserve to be THE TOP FLIGHT, we are a TOP FLIGHT Football Club, pure and simple. The players came down and did the lap of honour, everyone got covered with champagne and all the fans were ecstatic just how it should be.

It was a lovely trip home. Everyone was very happy and looking forward to being back where we belong, I couldn't wait, that was for sure everyone. We all went the next day to the Town Hall for the celebrations and we were not to be disappointed, the open top bus paraded through thousands and thousands of Town fans and the players looked a little worse for wear after the previous evening, who could blame them. We had the interviews and sing songs from the balcony as is the case in a joyous celebration like this is. Promotion is emotional especially for someone like Mr Sheepshanks who is Town through and through, he really got caught up in it all bless him. Anyway it all obviously has to come to an end and we were all very much looking forward to see what we could achieve in the coming season, would we be surprised? HERE'S HOPING EVERYONE!

Town Legend Marcus Stewart, pictured with Venetia (Colins Wife) outside Plymouth

Colin pictured with FA Cup, UEFA Cup and Play Off winner and manager of the year George Burley

Andrew, Colin, Marcus Stewart and Richard "The Cruncher" Moss

David Sheepshanks celebrates promotion

Andrew as a mascot at the Stadium of Light with David Sheepshanks

37 - INCREDIBLE SEASON 2000-2001

After what can only be described as the best season Town had had for years we were back with the BIG BOYS and it would certainly come to test us or would it I ask you lovely people. The first game of the season was away to Spurs and we got off to a dream start going 0-1 up early in the game through Venus, 36,148 fans, well most of them were stunned apart from the Town fans who were going mental!! The lead was not to last though and Spurs scored three times to eventually win 3-1, but it was not a bad performance overall on our return to the top flight.

The next game was at home to Man Utd in front of a full house of 22,007, not the 30,000 we can get in now, because Portman Road was still not developed as it is at the moment, the game was brilliant and the atmosphere was electric, it finished 1-1 with Wilnis scoring for Town and Beckham equalising for United, Ferguson said after the game it sounded more like 40,000 in the ground not 22,000, a fantastic tribute by a great manager. On the following Saturday we got our first win and it was against Sunderland, we won 1-0 thanks to a great run and finish from a marauding Bramble, it was just the tonic we needed and got us off to a decent enough start to the season, our next two games were against Leicester (A) and Aston Villa at home and we lost them both, a set back but we were playing some decent football so I was not too concerned, and also Stewart got off the mark as well in the loss to Villa, so that was good as well everyone. So we had got four points out of the first fifteen available but I was not too concerned as Like I say we were playing some decent stuff.

Our very next game, our sixth, took us to what can only be described as a cauldron, yes, you have guessed it Elland Road, now over the years we have not had the best record there, but certainly not the worst, so we went to Leeds Utd with a bit of hope. Leeds at this time were a very, very good side and especially at home in front of that load of fans of theirs, it can be difficult at times very difficult. The game started and at Leeds the last thing you want to do is give them a lead, and guess what after 4 minutes they were in front, but Town took the game to them and equalised after 12 minutes through Scowcroft, now Town were in the game and we went in front after half time with a goal from Jermaine Wright after and assist from Stewart, we held out until the final whistle and secured three good and very valuable points.

September was League Cup time and we drew Millwall, we lost 2-0 at the Den, only to thump them 5-0 in the second leg to go through 5-2 on aggregate, oh how Millwall love playing us in the cup competitions NOT. The next five league games saw us pick up eleven points out of fifteen, we were really taking to this league like ducks to water we really were. One of those wins was a 0-3 away win at Goodison Park, and how McGreal loved it as he scored up the Gladwys End to make it 0-1, now scoring at Everton for anyone is good, but when you are a Liverpool fan its a hundred times better trust me. Stewart got his normal goals, he got a brace and what finishes they were, he was really coming to the party, big time was Marcus Stewart. It was the start of November and the League Cup was back and we had a trip to Highbury to play Arsenal in round three, we beat them 1-2 with Clapham and Scowcroft seeing us through with no problems at all. Just after the Arsenal game we headed up to Newcastle to play Shearer and the boys at St James Park, a game I had to go to with all my wifes Geordie connections and all that. I absolutely love a trip to Newcastle Utd, that places is football crazy FULL STOP. I had my ticket in the corner at the top of that magnificent stand behind the goal, the other end to the Gallow Gate end at St James, Stewart scored for us but we eventually lost 2-1, but it was a great game, the next three games were all wins, Charlton (H) and Coventry and Man City away, nine points out of nine following the Goerdie defeat, we were flying absolutely flying folks, and playing excellently as well. Back to the League Cup and we had started to dream again of maybe winning the only trophy we hadn't won, we played Coventry at home and beat them 2-1 with Bramble and Johnson getting the important goals. We drew Man City (A) in the next round of the League Cup, but before we played them we had another three league games, of which we won two and lost one, against believe it or not Derby Country who were to finish 17th in the table, you can't win them all everyone, but one we did win was against Liverpool 0-1 at Anfield with Stewart rounding the keeper at the Kop End to secure three fabulous points against the side that was to finish third in the table, after beating Southampton at home 3-1, a game of which Armstrong scored his first Town goal, we then went to Maine Road for a fifth round league cup tie. Now we had already been there in the league and beat them, so we weren't duly worried about a cup tie there, and so it turned out, yes we had to go to extra time, but goals from Holland and Venus put us through to the last four of the League Cup again, surely we would make it this time, let's wait and see everyone, Birmingham City awaited us in the Semi Finals, surely we would, wouldn't we?

We had four games to play in the Premier League before the FA Cup, Man Utd (A), Chelsea (H), Spurs (H) and Sunderland (A) on New Years day, we won one, drew one and lost two, but after beating Spurs 3-0 at home before Christmas we went into the New Year not only expecting to stay up, but we were a very good bet to qualify for Europe and it certainly was not a joke either, we had been brilliant from the very first day of the season. In the FA Cup draw we got Morecambe, now I only thought people went there for a holiday, I certainly had never been there for a game of football. So off I went with a friend from Soham and his son and Andy came as well. The ground itself was very much nothing I had been used to over the years but it was an experience I must say, it was on Match of the Day in the evening, it was their cup final but it wasn't ours and we were very professional in beating them 0-3 in front of 5,923 fans, another ground ticked off my list, thank you FA.

We played Sunderland away in round four and went out 1-0, jarred off, yes, unhappy not overly, we were going so well in the league we all wanted to get back into that really, well I know I did 100%. The League Cup Semi Final first leg had already been played in early January and we had won 1-0 with a Stewart (pen) goal was it enough? I thought so at the time but St. Andrews is always a tough place to go, especially for an evening fixture. We had lost a couple of league games going into that semi final second leg, yes we had been on fire nearly all season but we had had a very small blip going into the Birmingham game, and you don't need that when St. Andrews is buzzing and full, trust me everyone. It was January nearly February cold, damp and horrible, the pitch was like my dad used to say, Southend with the tide out, mud, sand, everything but grass, it was made for Birmingham on the night. The game itself was a superb night for Horsfield he scored the first two goals which put Birmingham in the box seat until Scowcroft got us back to 2-2 on aggregate and still with a great chance of Wembley. It went to extra time and Horsfield completed his hat trick and another cruel goal for Ipswich came when Wright missed his kick and Johnston put it home to secure a final at Cardiff, so close but oh so far, that League Cup, well there's always next year I suppose!!

Everyone was lapping the league form up and the next two games at home were Everton (2-0) and Bradford on Sky TV, what a game that was, Bradford were at the bottom and came and made a real game of it and were 0-1 up but then after Burchill scored it was the Reuser show, he got two goals, the second a worldie into the top corner, my goodness what a player Reuser was, brilliant folks! Out of the last ten league games we won six, drew two, and lost two, we actually went into the last game at Derby with still a chance of the CHAMPIONS LEAGUE, yes Champions League you young Town fans we were that close, the previous game at home to Man City, we beat them 2-1 with goals from Holland and Reuser and that was enough to relegate Man City to the Championship, how times have changed everyone, well that's football for you! We finished fifth and qualified for the UEFA cup, an unreal season, thank you very much George and all the lads, you were all tremendous from start to finish THANK YOU!

Colin, Andrew and Ian at a Premiership press conference

38 - AFTER THE LORD MAYORS SHOW
2001-2002

After a fantastic season the previous season it really was a time for stability but unfortunately that was not to turn out to be the case, lots of projects were going on behind the scenes with the building of two new stands behind both goals, these projects had been going on for quite a while now, gone were the old North Stand and the Churchmans stand up the other end, to be replaced by two two tier stands renamed the Sir Bobby Robson Stand and the Sir Alf Ramsey Stand up the Churchmans end. Also new players were coming in and we signed Matteo Sereni and Finidi George, two players on very high wages, was that the right thing to do? TIME WOULD TELL EVERYONE!!

Although we had new players in, it was still the tried and trusted who played most of the games, Hreidarsson, McGreal, Venus, Clapham, Holland, Wright, Armstrong and Stewart, they were the mainstay of the squad. We were back in the UEFA Cup again after our fifth place finish the previous season, an achievement in itself, in the league we were to open up with Sunderland at the Stadium of Light in front of 47,370 fans, we competed really well but lost 1-0, so a lot to do as they say! Our first game at Portman Road was against Derby County, our first chance to see the new signings George and Sereni both did okay, but George was electric on the night, scored twice, we won 3-1 and all in all it was a tremendous debut by both of them. I thought this might be the turning point how wrong was I, oh my god from 25th August 2001 until the 17th December 2001 we didn't win another league game, we played fifteen games, we won none, drew six and lost nine, that was probably one of the worst runs I can remember in my lifetime in the top flight, AWFUL!!

Christmas though brought some good cheer and with Sixto Peralta now in the team we won seven out of the next eight league games, oh my goodness what a turnaround, was this a false dawn, we were soon to find out everyone! It gave everyone hope but as you know it's the hope that kills you, trust me! After beating Everton and looking good we then faced Liverpool at home in front of 25,608 we were thrashed 0-6 and it was just one of those games that you just wanted to end as soon as possible, it was totally embarrassing from start to finish.

The last twelve games we won one, drew three and lost eight of which the last was against Liverpool again and we lost 5-0, two games against the reds and we conceded eleven and scored none, we were down and we deserved to be, a shocking league season following a superb one, that's football as they say everyone! In the cups we obviously played in the UEFA Cup and maintained our UNBEATEN HOME RECORD in the competition, we drew Torpedo Moscow in the 1st round and won 3-2 on aggregate, Helsingborg were next and again we drew at home in the 1st leg but won away to go through 3-1 on aggregate. We then played Inter Milan in round three and what a tie, again at home in the first leg and we won 1-0 with Armstrong getting the winner, off we all went to Milan for the second leg, I went with a friend of mine from Soham, we had a great crack in Milan city centre with the other 9,000 Town fans, it was just like the good old days, fun, singing, beer and a brilliant time for everyone, it was superb. We had all day in Milan and about 6pm we set off for the San Siro Stadium, what a stadium it looks fantastic from the outside but not so good in the inside, but good anyway, its just being there you get the feeling I'm sure. Anyway to the game, we were obviously up against it, but we did our very best but unfortunately that was not enough and they won 4-1, 4-2 on aggregate and we were out, but a fantastic experience with an Armstrong penalty being our only goal, a great tie though for super Alun Armstrong.

In the League Cup it was very much the same old story. We had a favourable draw against Crewe in round three away, we won 2-3 with Reuser two, and Armstrong seeing us through. We drew Newcastle away in round four and we got thumped 4-1 with Darren Bent notching the goal, another league cup exit, were we destined to NEVER win this cup, it seems that way everyone!!

In the FA Cup another draw I definitely like Dagenham away, I hadn't been there so of course I had to make the trip, it was a bit of a cake walk really, we were all over them like a rash, and we played some decent football to win 1-4 in front of 5,949 at a very small but nice little ground at Dagenham, Peralta (2), Magilton and Stewart scoring the goals, McGavin playing for Dagenham that day,a good friend of mine is Steve McGavin, glad he lost though lol). In the next round we were at home to Manchester City and we got well and truly thumped 1-4 a game I would rather forget thank you. All in all an eventful season, roll on the following year, and back in the Championship!!!

39 - A LEGEND IS GONE 2002-2003

When a team is relegated it always takes time for everyone at the club to get going again, and that was no different for Ipswich Town, we had to hit the ground running, the only difference is when you have had a season like we had just had it is easier said than done. But we had to just get on with it, looking at the fixture list made you feel like, oh we are back in this league, but it's not all bad I suppose, a few new grounds and all that everyone!

We had Walsall away in the first league game, a game I went to and we were all happy enough at the end getting a 0-2 win with Ambrose and Marcus Bent scoring the goals in front of 5,253 fans, welcome back to the second tier folks!! Believe it or not we had qualified for the UEFA Cup again through the fair play awards and were handed a draw against Avenir Beggen, we played away in the 1st leg and Stewart earned us a 1-1 draw. The home leg was totally one way traffic and we won 8-1 (9-2 on aggregate) so our proud unbeaten home record was still intact thank goodness.

The UEFA cup was okay, but our bread and butter was the league and we followed up our impressive win at Walsall with a thumping 6-1 home win against Leicester with Counago (2), Holland (2), Ambrose and George scoring the goals, the crowd was 27,374 surely we were on to a good thing this season, or were we? The next six league games brought three draws and three defeats, one of the draws was a feisty derby versus Norwich which ended 1-1 with Counago being our hero on the day in front of 29,112 fans, it was a great atmosphere, but the result and results were not great to be honest. At the same time we were still in the UEFA Cup and we had a PROUD RECORD of never being beaten ever at home to protect, and against Smederevo we maintained it with a fine 1-1 draw with our dear old Armstrong getting the vital goal, we went over there and got a superb 1-0 win, courteous of a Marcus Bent (pen) and we were through yet again, brilliant for confidence I thought, I so hoped I was right.

This season was rather up and down and in the League Cup we drew Brighton and had no real problems putting them to the sword

3-1, Darren Bent, Counago and Ambrose scoring the goals, oh for a league cup success I hear you say! On the 6th October 2002 we went to Wimbledon and got a good 0-1 win with Ambrose scoring the winner, I thought that would probably be the catalyst for us to go on a good run of results and stop this horrible run of form we were having, but how wrong I was. Two days later on the 8th October 2002 we went to Grimsby Town and got beat 3-0 in front of 4,688 fans, it was an awful night, none more so for me because it was after this result that George Burley got the sack, a decision I always maintained was wrong and I still do to this day, totally wrong!! George Burley was an Ipswich man through and through, would the club regret it, I think the club probably still does if I'm being honest, 20 plus years service to the club, THANK YOU GEORGE. Anyway things had to carry on regardless and Mowbray was put into temporary charge a decision the fans and myself were okay with but it wasn't Mr Burley anymore and only time would tell how all of this was to affect the club long term. Mowbrays first game in charge was against Sheffield Wednesday at home and he got off to a decent start with a 2-1 win with Counago getting both goals, but attendances were dropping slightly, so the club really needed a good few results to get going again, easier said than done though.

The next three league games were to really decide if Tony Mowbray was to get the job or not, Reading (A), Burnley (H) and Gillingham (H) were to only bring one point out of nine and that really was the boards decision made up for them, we had to find another manager, pronto!! It was to be Joe Royle, at first some fans were a bit on the fence with the decision because of his Norwich City connections, but I wasn't. He was a superb manager who knew the game blindfolded, he would certainly do for me 100%, welcome "Big Joe".

If I remember correctly his first game was against Sloven Liberec at home a game we must not lose, we must protect our dear unbeaten home record in the UEFA Cup, no pressure then Joe! He was to be fine, we won 1-0 with Darren Bent scoring to maintain our superb home record, welcome to Portman Road Joe. Royles first league game was against Palace at home and it didn't go well, we lost 1-2 with Ambrose scoring, but we had to give the big man time and I'm sure he would be fine, hopefully. His next game was against Middlesbrough at home in the League Cup and we duly won 3-1, thing were looking up a little bit at this time everyone. After a 0-0 draw against Sheff Utd, we travelled over for the second leg of the UEFA Cup only to be beaten 1-0 on the night 1-1 (agg) only to lose 4-2 on penalties, what's new I hear you say! Out we go but as they say we must concentrate on the league big time!

In the seven league games up until Christmas, we won three, drew two, and lost two so not too bad but it really had to pick up if we were serious about promotion. In the League Cup we were seriously unlucky, we drew Liverpool away and we got a great 1-1 draw with Miller scoring the goal, only to go out 5-4 on penalties, again, I hear you all say! Anyway Christmas was upon us and we really needed to start putting the foot on the pedal and we certainly did, the three games over the Christmas period before the FA Cup we won all three, nine points out of nine, a great return of points, onwards and upwards! We drew Morecambe at home in the FA Cup and we easily won 4-0 with D. Bent (2), Clapham and Ambrose scoring. The 4th round was to be against our mates Sheffield Utd away and what a cup tie it was finishing 4-3 to them, but an unbelievable game nonetheless, a classic.

Our league form was still up and down and the next four games up until the 8th February saw us win two, draw one and lose one, it really wasn't very consistent but the football was exciting I've got to say. The club went into deep financial problems in 2003 and players like Stewart, Ambrose and Bramble left the club it really was oh so sad, I don't want to go deeply into all the financial stuff as I am not an accountant and don't know enough about it, all I will say is all of these problems were hurting myself very deeply because of my love of the club everyone, it was awful to witness.

Things did get a lot better in the derby at Carrow Road, we won 0-2 with dear old Wilnis and Darren Bent scoring the goals, the fans were going mental as usual. It's always SPECIAL TO BEAT THAT

LOT they know they will always be in our SHADOW - always. The last thirteen league games produced six wins, four draws, and three defeats, not a bad finish by big Joes blue and white army, but not quite enough to secure a place off place, we finished in seventh place, four points behind Forest but a gallant end to a very funny season.

The game of the season was against Sheffield Utd at home, we were 0-2 down and had also had Counago sent off in the first half as well, but we powered back with 10 men winning 3-2 with goals from Darren Bent (2) and Ambrose, a typical Joe Royle performance, truly tremendous, one of my favourite games for years.

40 - BIG PUSH BOYS PLEASE
2003-2004

The Joe Royle days had not started at all badly, yes we could have won more games but he was starting to build his own side, be it in quite difficult circumstances because of the clubs very bad financial situation, but he was doing a more than decent job in my opinion , and most other fans as well. Different players were coming in over the course of the last few months, Davis, Kuqi, Santos came in but of course we had lost one of our heroes in Matt Holland who went to Charlton Athletic, a very sad day indeed, all I can say is a very big thank you Matt Holland, a true gentleman, and a fantastic player and captain, thanks Matt.

The season was to start with a home game against Reading we had a decent crowd of 24,830 in and everything looked rosy, but we only drew the game 1-1 with a Miller (pen) so not the start we had been praying for, it was to get worse over the next five league games as we lost four and only drew with Coventry 1-1 at home, 2 points from eighteen, not promotion form at all, Joe needed to get things going and to be fair the big man certainly did. In amongst this dreadful start we had the annual attempt of doing something in that tournament called the League Cup and as always it started okay with decent win against Kidderminster, but we were knocked out at Notts County 2-1, no sleep was lost about that really as the league was the major objective as always for Ipswich Town.

Like I said, Joe had to pick the boys up in the league, we were playing some super football under Joe, scoring goals but also conceding loads as well. The next nine games saw us win eight games and only lost to Sunderland and that was 3-2 away at the Stadium of Light. We beat Wimbledon 4-1, Burnley 6-1 and Palace 3-4 in that mini run, my god it was great to watch, but not if you had a dodgy ticker, Joes teams were super, great attacking football just what everyone wanted to see, it was unreal at times scintillating!! It was all looking so good under Joe but the next ten games in the league up until Christmas were very up and down to say the least we only won three, drew four and lost three, one of which was against Norwich at home 0-2 in front of 30,152 fans, it was an awful result especially in front of a packed Portman Road enough said everyone. We had a fantastic win on Boxing day when Counago scored twice at Upton Park in a 1-2 win in front of 35,021, two clubs who should never be in the second tier of English football and was that a taster for later in the season who knows?

We had a third round FA Cup tie with Derby County in January and we put our fellow Championship club away quite easily 3-0 with Naylor, Miller and Kuqi scoring, what a signing Kuqi was becoming, so good up front with Bent they really were a force between them, fantastic!! Our cup run was to come to an abrupt end when we drew Sunderland away, we lost 1-2 Reuser on the score sheet. It was such a roller coaster of a season up and down most of the time as they say, the next ten games were to bring three wins, two draws and five defeats, not really promotion form, but in amongst that I saw one of the craziest games I have ever seen at Portman Road, it was against Crewe and it finished 6-4, it was an incredible game with Miller (2), Kuqi (2), Reuser and Counago getting the goals. I saw a similar game against Derby in the top flight once in the 70s, a totally astonishing game of football, typical Royle!!

We were now coming to the business end of the season and we all knew that we had to put in a fantastic end of the season run to make those play offs, the last ten league games produced six wins, two draws and two defeats, which enabled us to finish fifth and have a two legged semi final against West Ham a team we had lost once too, but also beaten them as well on Boxing Day at their place, so a very tight game was in store as we say.

Attendances had been brilliant at the end of the season, averaging probably about 27,000 in the run in, so it was no surprise when a gate of 28,435 turned up for the first leg at home, we won the game 1-0 with Bent scoring the winner, should we have won by more, you bet we should, but a wins a win and we went to Upton Park really fancying our chances. Now anyone who has been to West Ham Utd on a normal matchday knows its difficult, but when you go there and its a semi final second leg, and the tie is in the balance, you know you are in for a tough time and that is exactly how it turned out. Walking down to the ground from the car was intimidating to say the least, all the Irons fans were outside the pubs giving us dogs abuse, but what's new there then. The players came out and BUBBLES was being sung as loud as I had ever heard it, and my goodness I've been to Upton Park enough times trust me everyone. We had loads of great chances on the night but couldn't finish them off and West Ham took advantage and won 2-0 on the night, and 2-1 on aggregate another playoff defeat to go with all the others, it wasn't to be and another season in the second tier beckoned. Oh well we gave it our best shot I suppose, onwards and upwards folks!!

41 - GO AGAIN BOYS 2004-2005

After the heartbreak of the previous season surely Town could go one better this season. Joe brought in Jason De Vos at the back and we also had Darren Currie as well, two very different players of course, but in their own way very good additions indeed to the squad, we had the nucleus of a very good Championship side, let's go again boys.

The season opener was a home game against Gillingham, which we won 2-1 with goals from Naylor and Bowditch, Naylor was to become a pivotal figure in the '04-'05 season, a fantastic clubman was Richard. Although not a superb performance against Gillingham it was the start of a very good run of games, we won five of our first seven games, with one draw and one defeat, that coming against Derby County away 3-2 who eventually finished 4th in the table! Following the Town at this stage of my life was a real roller coaster, something I hadn't really tasted for a very long time, probably since the early Burley years, or even further back when Sir Bobby Robson first started at the club in the late 60s, early 70s. We had a League Cup draw in round one versus Brentford and won 2-0 only to go out to Doncaster, yes Doncaster 0-2, that was to prove a very good thing later on in the season trust me everyone! By Bye League Cup AGAIN!!

After the Derby defeat we were to go on a tremendous run as regards results, the football was exciting and everyone buying into Mr Royle, he was a true gentleman and an even better manager, we played the next sixteen league games and we won ten, drew five and only lost one, that was away at Stoke 3-2, we were really going well, and well in contention for going up automatically this season that was for sure. We were really putting together some fantastic runs in the league and leading up to Christmas we played nine games, winning five, drawing one, and losing three but they were all tricky games, Sunderland (A) 0-2 which I went to, Millwall (A) 1-3, and West Ham Utd (H) 0-2 in front of 30,003 fans on Boxing Day, a great atmosphere but an awful result against our play off rivals of '03-'04 season.

The FA Cup 3rd round was about again and we didn't really cover ourselves in much glory losing 1-3 at home to Bolton, revenge for Bolton I suppose they would say for the playoffs a few years previous. Darren Bent and Kuqi were a real handful in this particular season and they were such a deadly combination, defenders really never knew what to do with them, you had Bent with his extreme pace and you also had Kuqi with his unbelievable strength and both were clinical in front of goal, it all equals quality! The New Year started and we won three out of the next four with one draw against Reading away, I always loved that trip to Reading, we always took loads there and more times than not had a good time at their stadium. The last thirteen games in this superb season again saw us go up and down, we won five, drew four and lost four, it was typical Ipswich Town, losing games we were expected to win and finish third, two points behind Wigan, three draws in our last four games cost us big time!

So it was play offs Semi Finals AGAIN versus West Ham take two, we were at West Ham for the first leg and again a noisy Upton Park awaited us, but we dealt with it in a very good way in front of 33,723 noisy Irons fans, we drew 2-2 with goals from Walker (og) and Kuqi, surely we had done enough had we? Back to Portman Road four days later, and a very noisy crowd of 30,010 were waiting to propel Town to Wembley and hopefully the Premier League, how wrong we were, I couldn't believe it we lost 0-2, 2-4 on aggregate to say myself and my boys were gutted was the understatement of the season, oh well always next season as they say!!

42 - COULD WE MAINTAIN IT?
2005-2006

Supporting Ipswich Town has always been a way of life for myself, and after the previous season I was getting to the stage where I was asking myself "can we do this again"? I really wasn't sure to be honest we had so many ups and downs over the years I was really questioning whether we could maintain this form season after season., and its even more difficult of course when the money is tight if not running out altogether everyone! Most of the mainstays of the club were still there, but we were losing players mainly due to finance of course, Bent had gone of course and we were replacing players like Darren with players like Forster, Parkin and Lee etc. Lee coming later on in the season, we also gained Sito and our goalies now were Shane Supple and Lewis Price, it really was all change, but it had to be done with the state of affairs as they were at the time folks, very worrying indeed.

The season kicked off against Cardiff City at home and again the fans were not letting the club down at all, 24,292 turned up for the opener and witnessed a 1-0 win thanks to Forster, now Forster was always a player I had liked over the years, and I and the boys thought he would be the real deal for us at the time, we would see later on everyone! Talking of crowds, we averaged 24,251 in the '05-'06 season, an absolute credit to all Town fans everywhere as usual! Our start of the season was indifferent to say the least and an army of fans travelled to Loftus Road for the second game, only to see Town lose 2-1 with Parkin scoring the Town goal, great support as usual but this was to be an up and down season, the start certainly suggested it might be! The next three games against Leicester (A) 0-0 and Sheffield Wed (H) 2-1 and Millwall (H) 2-1 suggested we might just be more than okay to face Preston at home and get battered 0-4, that was a real wake up call for everyone, followed by another defeat at Sheffield Utd, like I said before very up and down, and the natives were starting to get more and more restless, and it was still only early September!

We had already played our league cup tie at Yeovil Town, not a game that lived long in my memory, there was a super crowd of 11,299 at the game, but Town just didn't turn up and we went out AGAIN 2-0 a shocking defeat. The League Cup just isn't for us everyone! The cups in general, be it the League Cup, or indeed the FA Cup were starting to become very difficult for Ipswich Town something I had NEVER known in my lifetime of following the Town, I was only ever used to last eight, last four or even cup finals, it was so frustrating to watch now for me. September 18th '05 Derby Day again folks, a crowd of 29,184 packed into Portman Road and again we were to lose to the enemy 0-1 and we all walked out of the North Stand thinking this might, just might be a very long season who knows?

As was usual Ipswich Town the very next game we went up to Leeds Utd, another club I'm not overly fond of, and we won 0-2 with Sam Parkin, yes PARKIN getting a brace, it was a fantastic result especially after just having been beaten by that lot down the A140, the crowd was 21,626, this at a club who always say they have one of the best supports in England, well I always say every club has fickle fans, and Leeds Utd are no exception at all. Where were we actually heading this particular season, no one really knew, the next three games we lost two and beat Crewe at home, it was absolutely so difficult to know what Town team was going to turn up from one game to the next, we needed to pick up and quickly too folks! Joe Royle was working on a shoe string budget and really under the circumstances I thought he was doing an okay job, but there is only so far you can take a squad when you have no real expenditure, Joe was doing really well all things considered and all the fans, me included loved him and his style of football as well by the way!

The next fifteen games up to the New Year brought only three wins, six draws and six defeats, not at all promotion form, more like relegation form, something had to change and quickly! The FA Cup saw us go out with a whimper again against Portsmouth at home 0-1, we just couldn't get going in any way at all in cup competitions again it seemed, it was so unlike Ipswich Town to be going out of cups so early, it was becoming an awful habit actually, not nice at all.

We had to get our foot down on that pedal in the league, and the New Year brought a bit of optimism out of the next nine games we won five, drew three and only lost one to Wolves away, so were kind of back on track, well we thought we were everyone! In the last eleven league games we managed to win only two, we drew three and lost six, it just was not good enough and Town finished the season in 15th place, as low as I could ever remember in years, we really were becoming an average second tier side, so sad especially for my generation who had seen so much better, it was awful really, but like I said how on earth could you blame Joe Royle. I certainly didn't, it was a club problem in my eyes folks. His last game was against Plymouth Argyle away, we lost 2-1 with Forster getting the goal on the 11th May 2006 Mr Royle was gone to be replaced by club legend Jim Magilton, a very popular choice indeed but so sad to see Joe depart he was loved by everyone including me, "Thanks Joe".

43 - SUPER JIM MAGILTON 2006-2007

After the sad exit of big Joe Royle, Town decided to appoint from within, and it was to be the mercurial Jim Magilton, now Jim was a fellow that always wore his heart on his sleeve and I and most Town fans absolutely loved that, he was a winner, anyone who witnessed that Bolton semi-final in the playoffs knew exactly what Town meant to him, he was a very popular choice indeed at the time everyone. Jim was enrolled as a player still, but decided to retire from the game and put all his concentration into being a manager, that was a surprise, but I always thought it was the best way forward for him to be a success at the club. Finances were still not great at the club, and Jim had to wheel and deal in the market, just like dear old Joe Royle had to for so long, Bruce, Harding, Legwinski came in followed later by Roberts, David Wright and Walters to name just a few, other deals were done but they were the main ones during the season.

Crowds were still very good at the time, and the club could never ever blame the fans, they stood by the team through thick and thin and were still doing so, fair play to them. We opened the season with a home game against Palace, it didn't go well for Jim Magilton, he was his usual self on the touchline kicking every ball but to no avail, we lost 1-2 with Forster getting our goal, it was to be his last as he and Parkin were soon to be transferred out of the club, Lee, Haynes, Clarke and Walters to be the men who stepped into the side at different times during the season. The next three league games also proved to be quite testing and against Wolves (A) 1-0, Leicester (A) 3-1 and Hull (H) 0-0 Town were to only register one point, so one point out of the first twelve, not good at all, I felt for Jim as we all knew exactly how he was feeling, you could see it a mile off, we needed a result and no more than Jim did, he needed it ASAP especially after last season. It didn't get any better in the next game, we drew Peterborough in the League Cup at London Road and it didn't go well as we drew 2-2 and lost 4-2 on penalties, OMG, have we ever won on penalties apart from against luton that night at Portman Road, so the League Cup was over again at round one, nothing new there then folks!

We needed points and wins and over the next ten games, we won six, drew one and lost three, the defeats coming against Colchester (A) 1-0, WBA (H) 1-5 and Preston (H) 2-3, the defeats against Colchester Utd and WBA were shocking results, my goodness the coaching staff had an enormous job on with this squad, things had to change sooner rather than later. Magilton could never be questioned for effort ever, his next game was against Southend at Roots Hall, a fixture I always enjoyed going to, we won 1-3 with Clarke, Legwinski and Lee on the scoresheet, a gate of 11,415 were there mainly because of our fantastic away support, our support was never in question ever. We followed that away win with a hammering of Luton (H) 5-0 again Lee (3), Legwinski and Peters. Was this to be a turning point? Who knows with Town at that point everyone? Form was very up and down at this point and leading up to the local derby against Norwich City we had lost another couple of games, so not good at all when Town had the Canaries in Town in the middle of November 27,276 turned up for the derby and what a derby day it turned out to be, Jim Magilton had the boys pumped right up and we played so well to win 3-1 with Canary crusher Haynes getting two and the other coming from Legwinski, it was party time, as it always was when we beat that lot it was pure heaven, get the pints in lads and lasses.

After the Norwich game I said to my boys surely this is the turning point of our season, WRONG! We could never get a solid run together at any point in the season, we seemed to always have a dip just after a high, I just couldn't work it out if I'm being honest. The next nine games leading up until Christmas we only won three, drew two and lost four, it just wasn't good enough and if we didn't pick it up soon we would be a mid table side yet again, we all including Jim Magilton knew that 100%. I was more than pleased it was January and we could look forward to my favourite competition, the FA Cup, we had drawn Chester City which was good because I hadn't been there. I went with Andrew in the car, it was a small ground, but nice and compact, the game itself wasn't brilliant but we didn't get beaten, and finally drew 0-0, so a replay at Portman Road was to be played in ten days time, and we go through winning 1-0 with Richards scoring the winner. League form was still so inconsistent we had a local derby against Colchester at home which was attended by 28,355 an unreal support for a team doing so badly at the time, we did manage to win 3-2, Lee, Legwinski and Haynes on the score sheet again, but surely this was just papering over the cracks, that what I thought anyway, along with a lot of other people. At least we were still in the FA Cup and we had drawn Swansea at home in found four, we beat them 1-0 with a penalty from Lee, a very good win which kept our interest going for a while anyway, and a nice tie away to Watford to look forward to in February.

In the league in February either side of the Watford cup tie we had player four, lost four and not even scored a goal, we were struggling quite badly, I felt for Magilton because I and everyone else knew what it meant to him, he just wasn't getting the rub of the green at all, it was so sad to watch to be honest. At the middle of February we went to Watford in the FA Cup and as usual we took a huge following with us, it was only the referee who was absolutely awful on the day who cost us at least getting a replay, some of his decisions were atrocious and we lost 1-0, when on any other day we would have won the game, let alone drawn it.

Back to the league and we finished actually not to bad at all, out of the last twelve games, we won seven, drew two and lost only three, so a decent finish to the season, but the season itself was a big let down, we finished 14th in the table, not really acceptable for a club like Ipswich Town, but hey ho, we finished higher than Norwich, who finished sixteenth. The season was over, but my oh my how we had to improve in the summer if this wasn't to be repeated again "Come on Super Jim".

44 - MUST DO BETTER 2007-2008

After a few seasons of underachieving, we all thought this could well be the season that Jim Magilton could well get it right, he had brought Counago in and had what looked to be a very attacking side, what with Lee and Haynes in the squad as well. Town had a solid looking back four with De Vos and Bruce forming a good partnership in the middle, along with David Wright and Dan Harding as the full backs, it looked decent, very decent indeed. The team was changing all the time and Garvan, Miller and Roberts were doing a good job in the middle, along with Haynes and Quinn. Alexander was brought in as goalkeeper from Cardiff, Miller from Sunderland, to be followed later in the season by Quinn from Sheff Utd, Sumulikoski from Bursaspor and David Norris from Plymouth, a great signing by super Jim.

The season kicked off at home to Sheffield Wednesday and what a start, Jims side made good and won 4-1, with goals from Alan Lee (2), Roberts and Counago, we were playing fast attacking football, just what everybody wanted, a bit like in the Joe Royle style I thought, gates were still very good considering how the club had fared over the last few seasons, still over the 20,000 mark most weeks! We followed the Wednesday game up with a League Cup tie at MK Dons, we drew 3-3 and lost 5-3 on penalties, a game which my son Ian went to with his mates, I suppose in the bigger scheme of things it wasn't the end of the world as the league was by far the more important competition, we could 100% concentrate on that now at least until the FA Cup kicks off.

David Sheepshanks was still the Chairman during the '07-'08 season but as I've spoken about before, the running of the club was getting more and more difficult by the season, if not by the day! It was difficult times for everyone at the club, no more than for Mr Magilton who under the financial pressures was doing an adequate job, or he was in my mind everyone! The first twelve games of the season including the Sheffield Wednesday game, we won six, drew three and lost three, so twenty one points out of thirty six, not too bad a start at all, enough to give Jim breathing space anyway. Derby time was upon us again and Town went the short trip down the A140 to play Norwich, it was nearly bonfire night, so we could expect fireworks, well it was your typical local derby with Lee and Counago scoring the goals in a 2-2 draw, a fair enough result in front of 25,461 at Carrow Road. A defeat at promotion contenders Sheffield Utd was followed by a convincing 6-0 home win against Bristol City with Walters (3), Wright , Miller and Counago on the scoresheet, it was so entertaining to watch Lee, Walters and Counago in the same side, we were fast becoming a very joyable attacking side to watch, it was superb!

A bit like previous seasons we were up one day and down the next, that is what supporting Ipswich was generally getting to be like, it's the hope that kills you as they say! The next eleven games leading up to the FA Cup we won four, drew two and lost five! Not too brilliant a record at all, as we say we must do better. In the FA Cup we drew Portsmouth from the Premier League and we had a gate of 23,446 for the tie, we were to lose 0-1 in a game we deserved a replay at worst, but it was not to be and Portsmouth went on to lift the FA Cup at Wembley beating Cardiff City, so another year of Cup football came to an end, something we were getting very used to by now, so, so frustrating especially for my generation and older of course! We were still very well placed in the league and three draws and a win set us up very nicely for a game against Watford at home in February, a game we really desperately wanted to win as they were there or thereabouts and it was always going to probably come down to the wire between several clubs, Watford and Ipswich included who was going to make the playoffs, so quite a vital game. 24,227 supporters were at Portman Road to see us get beat 1-2 with Walters scoring the goal, I remember saying to my boys what a body blow that could turn out to be, we would have to wait and see…

Two wins followed against Palace and Blackpool with Sumulikoski getting his first goal for the club, a similar event happened for Norris at Southampton a couple of games later, great to see different players getting their share of the goals. Form was so very much up and down, and it all culminated in Town losing 2-0 at Colchester Utd, a totally embarrassing result to say the least, but it summed the season up really, were we good enough? Time would eventually tell us folks! After the Colchester United game we had five games to play, of which we won two, and drew three, one of which was against Norwich City at Portman Road and my goodness did we need the points, we got them courtesy of a 2-1 win with yet another Norwich (og) this time coming from Pearce, the other goal was Haynes the Canary Crusher, he notched again to send Portman Road wild with excitement 29,656 fans thought we were going to make it, and to be honest so did I.

We went into the last game against Hull City knowing we must win, and win we did 1-0 with Lee getting our goal, the only problem was the results went against us and we missed out on the playoffs by one point, it was soul destroying, but what can you do everyone? We finished eighth with 69 points, better than the previous season, but ultimately not good enough, it was second tier football again the next season folks!

45 - NEW CHAIRMAN 2008-2009

By this time, the club had a new owner, Mr Evans who had bought the business in 2007, he was to become our new chairman this season taking over from the long standing, and in my opinion very good chairman David Sheepshanks, I say that on the back of he was always very helpful to myself personally especially after I lost my father, he was a total gentleman and will always be missed at the club by myself, he also allowed me to put a plaque up on the back of what was the Pioneer stand and I will be forever grateful to him for that "Thank You David".

Of course when Mr Evans gained ownership of the club everybody including myself thought lovely jubbly this is a new era, loads of money and all that goes with it, Premier League etc, we would find out in the coming weeks, months and years if that was to be the case, I will leave that for later everyone!! We had fans totally and utterly excited by the whole takeover to the extent they were seen flashing £20 notes at the Barclay end at Norwich City, that went well did it? It was all tongue in cheek stuff, but not an entirely good idea looking back.

Jim had to hit the ground running this season in my opinion, he made some decent signings in the summer bringing Richard Wright back to the club, as well as signing McAuley, Thatcher, Stead, Campo and Civelli. Ambrose and Dos Santos came on loan as did Bialkowski from Southampton. We ousted several players that season including Williams, Wilnis, de Vos, Legwinski, Sito, Roberts, Lee, Naylor, Nick Pope (we free transferred to Bury Town, that went well didn't it!). All in all I think most fans including myself thought the business done was more than adequate, we would find out as the season progressed everyone!!

We opened up at home to Preston in front of 22,307 fans who were so looking forward to our new era, it didn't start well, we were beat on home soil 1-2 with Lisbie scoring his first goal for the club, a disappointing start, but hey we've still got 45 games to play. The League Cup was to be a welcome distraction and we played Orient at home and won 4-1, Haynes (2), Miller and Lee on target, surely we must do something in this competition one day? That put us in good heart for the long trip to Burnley, Turf Moor, which was one of my favourite grounds in England, history to it, and all that, we won 0-3 Trotter, Lisbie, and Jordan (og) to seal us all three points, perhaps it just might be our season, who knows?

We needed to find some consistency in our game, but unfortunately, that doesn't always bode well with Ipswich Town, and alas, we lost our next two games against Wolves at home and away to Watford, two teams who would be up at the top end nearly all season long. Oh how I wanted Jim Magilton to succeed, as did every other Town fan, he was as passionate as just about anyone who had ever managed Ipswich Town, everybody loved him, and like myself, probably still does, he was a fans manager was Jim 100%. In the League Cup we played another two rounds, firstly at Colchester at home in round two, a game we won 2-1, and Wigan again at home where we lost 1-4 well it was the League Cup after all everyone and we went out for another year.

We needed to get our heads down and really put together a consistent run in the league now, especially now we were out of the League Cup, but unfortunately that was not to be the case because in the next eight games we only managed to win two, we drew five and lost one, by far too many draws, we were slipping too far behind too soon AGAIN!! We got into that same old Ipswich mould of winning a few, drawing a few and losing not many, but at the end of the day that sort of form is only going to get you playoffs at the very best, something our fans would take obviously, but top two is really what a club the size of Town is desperately after.

Derby day was here again and what with Norwich struggling somewhat in the league, we all thought it would be quite a comfortable day, we were all wrong, we got beat 2-0, something I never really witnessed too often when I first supported Town, but it was just starting to become more than a once in a while scenario, I hated losing to them, and still do with a passion!! It was so in and out leading up to Christmas, we really couldn't get that promotion form going. There was always a defeat in us somewhere, we lost on Boxing Day at home to Birmingham 0-1, then beat Derby away 0-1 with Jon Walters scoring, a great day out for everyone!

FA Cup 3rd Round day was upon us and we drew Chesterfield at home, we won 3-0 in front of 12,524 fans, I couldn't remember many FA Cup ties at home with so few fans in the ground, a sign of the times as they say I suppose. We went to Stamford Bridge in the fourth round and we got beat 3-1, but we gave a very good account of ourselves in front of 41,137, Bruce scored our goal much to the away fans delight! Either side of losing to Chelsea we had played two league games against Palace (A) and Barnsley (A) and we won them both 1-4 and 1-2 respectively, but again the next three saw us draw two and lose one at Swansea, it just was not good enough and something had got to change very quickly or I could sense the worst maybe for Jim Magilton, especially now we had Mr Evans in charge, I prayed for Jim to pick it up, but would he, time would tell everyone. We won on my birthday (18th Feb - same day as Mr Robson by the way) against Forest, we won 2-1, and I always loved it when we won on my birthday because the evening was always so much more enjoyable especially for my wife Venetia.

The next ten games in the league brought two wins, four draws and four defeats, not good going into a home East Anglian Derby match, but funnier things have happened folks. Before the derby Dos Santos had come in and what a signing he proved to be, he was quick, direct, and oh my god how he could finish, he was simply brilliant! We had 28,274 in Portman Road for the Norwich City game and what a game, it finished 3-2 to us with Quinn, Stead and a Dos Santos penalty, the atmosphere that day was on a different level, it was just so nice to get one over them, was it enough to keep Jim Magilton his job, NO IT WASN'T. Jim was sacked after the Norwich game and replaced with Roy Keane who saw the last two games out both wins 0-3 at Cardiff City and at home to Coventry City a 2-1 win in front of 27,225 fans was it to be a marriage made in heaven, who knows?

Ipswich finished in ninth place, 8 points off the play offs, was it hard on Jim Magilton? I honestly thought it was everyone, was it something we were going to face and put up with? Time would always tell, this was Ipswich under new ownership, very different to the Cobbold and Sheepshanks days, that was for sure.

On the 31st July 2009, Ipswich Town lost one of our greatest ever managers in Sir Bobby Robson, he died a day before my Ian & Jo got married, something I will never forget. He truly gave myself, my dad and my family some of the best days of our lives.

Thank you Bobby, R.I.P sir.

46 - ROY KEANE, RIGHT OR WRONG
2009-2010

Would this be the season we eventually cracked the Champagne bottles open and got back to where all Town fans really thought we belonged, it really was the million dollar question but I truly believed that most Town fans were quite excited at first when Mr Evans brought Roy Keane into the Portman Road hot seat. Rightly or wrongly I initially thought it was a top appointment, great career at Man Utd and Forest and obviously had learnt a great deal under the management of the great Sir Alex Ferguson and of course the great Brian Clough, was I to be correct, well time would certainly tell as they say everyone. Most people were excited about the fact we were spending money again, but it's how you spend it, spend it wisely and you are on to a winner, spend if foolishly and you end up looking for another job, it remained to be seen how Keane was to end up? Keane brought in Delaney, Martin, Priskin, Edwards, Brown, O'Connor and Brian Murphy, he also brought in Colback, Begovic, John, Rosenior and later in the season Daryl Murphy and David Healy. He also god rid of 14 players and loaned out eleven, my god Keane meant business let's hope it worked out for him everyone.

The season kicked off at Coventry City and like all managers you hope to get off to a reasonable start, as usual Town were encouraged by a decent away support, but the team were beaten 2-1 with Jon Walters on target for Ipswich. The gates were still very good at Portman Road considering how the side had done in recent seasons averaging around the 20,000 mark, we had 22,454 in for the first home game against Leicester City, but again we huffed and puffed and drew the game 0-0 we just had to start getting results or the pressure would mount and mount on Keane, that was for sure, Keane continued doing his Sky Sports interviews about anything and everything and one thought was this the real reason Evans brought him in to manage Ipswich Town? I was really starting to believe that it was you know, every time he was on the television there he was in front of the Marcus Evans logo, good publicity for your company one hundred percent, he was talking about United and Ireland more than he was about Town, it was getting to me and loads of other Town fans as well, trust me.

The next twelve league games produced no wins, seven draws and five defeats, it simply was just not good enough, that was fourteen games from the start of the season without a win. I questioned if he really ever wanted to be here in the first place and as time went on I certainly got my answer everyone!! We hadn't even won in the League Cup in August because we only managed to beat Shrewsbury on penalties after drawing 3-3 then went out in round two to Peterborough Utd 2-1 at London Road, absolutely awful folks! We finally got our first win of the season on the 31/10/2009 at home to Derby with no other than David Wright getting the winner in what was the our seventeenth game of the season, it was great to win but my goodness what an underwhelming start to any season, the fans were not happy and who could blame them, four more draws out of the next six games, but at least we won a couple against Cardiff and Blackpool, it was just papering over some enormous cracks, our record under Keane was poor, very poor indeed. Christmas had arrived and we had won three games in the league, this had got to be nearly as low as I could remember watching my favourite football club, we lost again on Boxing Day 3-1 at Palace, only to beat QPR at home on the 28th December to ease the pain a little with Walters and Stead (2) getting the goals in front of 25,349 almost happy Town fans certainly relieved Town fans that was for sure.

Blackpool were drawn in the FA Cup and Bloomfield Road was the destination for our wounded squad, we won 1-2 with Colback and Garvan securing a fourth round draw against Southampton at St. Marys ,we lost 2-1 another year of cup anguish everyone! Now we were out of both cups we simply had to start getting points in the league in our second half of the season. Out of the twenty three league games, we won only eight, we drew eight and lost seven to finish a very disappointing fifteenth in the table with only 56 points, Keane, the jury was very much out on him, with all the money Keane had spent to finish 15th in the Championship was just not good enough for a club like Ipswich Town, Mr Keane, you must IMPROVE and quickly my dear friend end of!!

47 - THE GOOD AND BAD OF IPSWICH TOWN FC 2010-2011

Season 201011 was upon us and Roy Keane had to start well, especially after such an underwhelming season as he had had in the previous campaign, it had to be good, fans were getting more than a bit fed up of his interview after interview and nothing to show on the pitch. Again he had brought in a few additions Hourihane, Kennedy, Fulop, Scotland and Drury were all signed with a few good loan additions as well namely Townsend, O'Dea, Livermore, Colback, Fallon and later on in January we got Bullard and Dyer in as well. Keane also ousted 10 players which included Trotter, both Wrights (David and Richard), Balkenstein, Upson, Bruce, Garvan, Walters and Stead, I prayed he knew what he was doing because to be honest I wasn't convinced.

We opened up the season at Middlesbrough and to be honest it went well with Town winning 1-3 at the Riverside Stadium in front of 21,882 of which there were a fair few of our lot who had travelled to see a fine win with Smith, Priskin and Stead getting the goals, a start Keane certainly needed trust me! We had quite a good start to the season to be fair, in the next 9 games, we won four, drew three and only lost two, a good points return of 18 out of the first 30 points and sitting fifth in the table. In that tenth game of the season we had played Leeds Utd, beat them 2-1 with a certain Bruce getting sent off too, its always lovely beating Leeds Utd and this occasion was certainly no different at all. It was all going very decently in the league but unfortunately in the twelve games leading up to Christmas we only won three, drew none and lost nine, including a shameful display at Norwich City when we got beat 4-1, with Holt getting a hat trick and Hoolahan getting the other, Delaney scored for Town before getting sent off in the 39th minute, GAME OVER. and not just for Town, more on that later everyone!!

Ipswich had lost a couple of games because of the weather over Christmas, but the New Years day game was on a 1-1 draw at Coventry, but it was to be the next game a 0-1 defeat to

Nottingham Forest that was to cost Keane his job, he had already fallen out with our fans with little spats here and there so that was not very good but more importantly his record at Town was awful, and with Delaney scoring an own goal and also Leadbitter getting sent off it really did feel like the end for Keane and so it was, he was sacked after the Forest game and Ian McParland was put in charge for the forthcoming couple of fixtures, a couple of cup games, he led us into a third round FA Cup tie versus Chelsea, of which we got firmly demolished 7-0 and the first leg of a League Cup semi final versus Arsenal at Portman Road, more on that later, Keane lasted as Ipswich Town manager for 81 games, a shocking statistic considering our history in never very often sacking our managers, this really was starting to be the bad of Ipswich Town FC to be honest folks!! So a new appointment was made and it was to be Mr Paul Jewell from Derby County, but he had not managed actually for some time before he came to Ipswich, so fingers crossed Jewell could turn it all around, here's hoping everyone!

His first game was against Millwall away, what a treat for a new manager, and it didn't go to plan as we lost 2-1 at the New Den with Priskin on target, surely better was to come, we would see in the future. Jewells next six games saw him win four and draw two, surely we were at last on the up, wrong, the next six games saw us win one and draw one and lose four, same old, same old, I hear you say, but surely we must give the man a chance and so we did, four wins out of the next five games the other being a draw against Middlesbrough leading into the derby game versus Norwich at home, what a disaster that turned out to be, we lost 1-5 the biggest derby defeat I had ever witnessed and this was followed up four days later with a 4-1 defeat at Swansea and had we made the right call on Jewell, GOD KNOWS everyone it certainly didn't seem it to me or a lot of other Town fans for that matter, we finished off the season with a 2-1 win against Preston, a 4-2 defeat at Leicester Leadbitter (pen) and Wickham scoring the last goal of a very very up and down season.

I left the good of the season to last because just for once we had a great run in the League Cup, Exeter 2-3 (aet), Crewe 0-1 (aet), Millwall 1-2, Northampton 3-1 and WBA 1-0 in the fifth round brought a Semi Final against our old friends from Arsenal to Portman Road. A crowd of 29,146 came to watch as Ipswich contained and played very well against Arsenal and we duly got our winner in the 78th minute through Priskin, a much deserved victory and something to take to the Emirates in the second leg. We took thousands to Arsenal for the return leg and we were holding on gallantly until the 61st minute when Bendtner opened the scoring for Arsenal, we then conceded further goals in the 64th and 77th minutes to lose 3-0 and 3-1 on aggregate, my dream of seeing my beloved Ipswich Town FC in a League Cup final over again, but a tremendous effort by our side and who knows, there's always next season as we all say "well played lads".

Summary of the season - 13th in the Championship, just not good enough in a nutshell Mr Evans.

48 - THE IPSWICH LOYAL DESERVE BETTER 2011-2012

After what had been several underwhelming seasons this was to be my tenth consecutive season watching second tier football, something I really had never been accustomed to in all my life of supporting the Town, it was a theme that was to continue for a lot longer, but I wasn't to know that obviously. Paul Jewell really had to hit the ground running this season, because his record since joining the club the previous season of ten wins out of twenty one league games was not bad, but an improvement was hopefully on the cards if we were to be taken seriously for promotion. There was loads of transfer activity at the club this season with Wickham going to Sunderland for £8.1 million pounds, this enabled Jewell to get in a couple of million pound players himself in Chopra and Jay Emmanuel Thomas, we also signed Cresswell from Tranmere who turned out to be a bargain at £240,000, a superb left foot had Aaron.

We opened the season at Ashton Gate home of Bristol City and we won 0-3 with goals from Chopra (2) and Martin, oh my god had we actually cracked it, no was the simple answer everyone because three days later we played Northampton at Portman Road and we lost 1-2 after leading the game, bye bye League Cup once more! We followed that game up with three defeats out of the next four games including a 2-5 home defeat to Southampton and a totally embarrassing 7-1 loss at Peterborough United, a game I still regard as the most awful performance in my supporting Ipswich Town lifetime, it was shocking, we went 0-1 up only to have two players sent off, it was a car crash from 23 minutes onwards, Peterborough didn't even score their first goal until the 30th minute and finished up scoring seven!! It was all so up and down under Jewell and once more we gave the fans hope when we won five out of the next eight games which took us back up to sixth place in the table, heady heights indeed folks. In that mini-run we beat Leeds Utd 2-1, with a last minute goal from Andrews, always a treat to beat Leeds Utd especially like that, we also beat

Coventry 3-0, West Ham 0-1, Brighton 3-1 and Portsmouth 1-0, was it a false dawn, time would tell as usual with Town!

Just after everyone was thinking maybe playoffs this season "disaster struck" the next seven games were all to end in defeat, perhaps the Christmas turkey was not going to taste as nice as we thought it might, who knows? A couple of nice wins just before Christmas 3-5 at Barnsley and a 1-0 home win versus Derby eased the pain somewhat but a lot of work had to be done after the Christmas break to make this a successful season that was for sure. It was all starting to become a slog for Ipswich and a defeat in the 3rd round of the FA Cup to Hull didn't help, we would lose a couple and then lose three or four games that is exactly how it was under Mr Jewell, we won five out of six after Christmas and produced steady results but not enough wins under our belt to sustain anything like a play off place in fact we finished fifteenth again, this was not good enough, but to be honest we had become very much a mid table second tier football club, something I found very hard to accept, but hey ho there's always next season.

49 - BIG MICK COMES IN 2012-2013

Once more after another miserable season in the Championship finishing mid table change was needed and we certainly got that, in total over the 2012/2013 season eleven players were signed including Chambers, Taylor, Reo-Coker, Mings, Nouble and Wordsworth, seventeen players were loaned including Murphy, Wellens, Campbell, Higginbotham, McGoldrick, Stearman, Henderson and Tabb, sixteen players were transferred and six loaned out, it was a complete change all round, we could only hope and pray it world work out. Paul Jewell in my opinion was a good man, but good men don't always succeed.

He needed a fast start to the season, starting with Blackburn Rovers at home, we drew 1-1 with an 82 minute (og) by Lowe giving us a point, we followed that up with a very handy three points at Watford on the Tuesday night, courtesy of a 90th minute Chopra goal, oh boy, how we all celebrated, there is NOTHING like a last minute goal away from home, four points from six was very promising, was it to last who knows everyone!! We played two games that season in the League Cup winning 3-1 at home to Bristol Rovers before bowing out again early doors to Carlisle Utd 2-1 away, conceding in the 90th and 99th minutes, we are destined never to win this trophy as far as I see it folks!!

After a decentish start to the league season, our next eleven games were to become a nightmare, not just for the fans but more importantly Paul Jewell, we played Blackpool and got beat 6-0 at Bloomfield Road and after that we lost another seven times drawing three and winning none, the home defeat to Sheffield Wednesday on 27th October 2012 was to be Jewells last game before he got sacked, Hutchings took over for a brief spell, but then Mick McCarthy was appointed as our new manager on the 1st November 2012, a very experience manager with a very good CV behind him in professional football, I was pleased with him coming in as were a lot of Town fans at the time, we needed a firm hand to steady this ship, that was for sure. It was a weird period just after Mick took over because we beat Birmingham away 0-1, then lost 5-0 at Palace, then beat Burnley 2-1 and then lost 6-0 to Leicester, where was this all going it was so hard to predict from one game to another. Attendances at Portman Road by this time had started to fall, we were probably only averaging about 17,000 at this time, but it wasn't surprising because the football at times was shocking at best everyone!

My eldest sons Ians birthday was upon us and we played Peterborough Utd at home on his birthday and we drew 1-1 with DJ Campbell netting for Town, we needed a run of results before Christmas and we duly goth them, after the Posh game, we played seven games up to the New Year and we won five, drew one and only lost one game away at Leeds United, Mick had certainly made a difference in how we played especially defensively that was for sure. A home defeat to Brighton 0-3 was followed by a trip to Aston Villa in the cup, not a favourite ground of mine in the FA Cup especially after losing a Semi Final there to Man City in 1981, a game we should NEVER have lost, anyway the game with Villa was a very good game and we went in front courtesy of a Chopra goal, only to be pegged back by Villa in the second half, Bent and Weimann scoring for Villa, the last goal coming in the 83rd minute, a right sickener for all Town fans at Villa park.

Mick McCarthy was not everybody's cup of tea, but I liked him when he first came in, he gave us stability if nothing else and in the second half of the season we played twenty games under Mick, winning eight, drawing six and losing six, not bad after what he had taken on I thought!! We finished fourteenth, not too bad considering!

50 - STABILITY PLEASE MICK!
2013-2014

Mick was slowly but surely building his side he signed McGoldrick, Tabb and Murphy permanently and also got in Anderson, Gerken, Lee, Veseli, Berra and Stephen Hunt on free transfers, say what you like about McCarthy but he was very good at spotting a bargain or two. He also brought in Tunnicliffe, Graham, Green, Richardson, Henshall and Jonny Williams, Williams was to finish up very much a crowd favourite at Ipswich Town, a very good signing indeed, as were quite a few of the other players he had inherited. Money by this time had increasingly become very tight indeed, especially after the amount of cash Roy Keane had squandered on most of his so called decent signings, in my opinion Keane crucified our club and now the likes of Mick McCarthy were left to sort it all out, wheeling and dealing wherever he could and to be fair he was making a decent fist of it to be honest, he had got a decent squad together for next to nothing really, good on him!! Also Mick had started to get rid of a lot of the misfits at the club especially players like Chopra, Martin, Lee Barratt and Taylor, what a failure Taylor was, probably one of the worst signings in the last 25 years in my opinion folks, but the clearouts had to be done for the club to have any chance at all of going forwards. We had the nucleus of a good side now especially with Murphy and McGoldrick upfront so we all looked forward to a good season.

We opened up at Reading, one of those new stadiums that all look the same, no character at all in other words, so off we went down to Reading with loads of fans as always, only to get beaten 2-1, Tabb putting us in front only for Reading to score right on half time and then getting the winner in the 75th minute, a goal scored by Guthrie it was disappointing, but we go again as they say. We followed the Reading game with a League Cup tie at Stevenage, we lost 2-0 after conceding two goals in the second half, our cup records by this time were nothing short of shocking and no result in the cup competitions surprised me anymore, always next season eh! In a way I actually thought it was a blessing in disguise as we just had to get our act together in the league, we had been in the Championship up to this point over 11 years, shocking for a club the size of ours and a club that boasted success in Europe to boot.

Next up was Millwall at home and we got a good win with three second half goals an OG, Anderson and Hewitt sealing the win we were up and running or so we thought, come on this is Ipswich we are talking about here everyone. The next two games were both defeats, we lost 1-0 at QPR, then we lost at home to Leeds Utd 1-2, a team apart from Norwich City I hate losing to, it all goes back to the days of Bremner, Giles, Clarke and Charlton days, yes you have guessed it "DIRTY LEEDS" and my goodness they were dirty trust me, I despise losing to them 100%. My club, your club were down in seventeenth place we had to get some wins, and get some wins we did, we got three victories out of the next five games and that got everybody feeling a lot better, no more so than the players themselves, we really needed it, especially if we were going to challenge for the playoffs in May. In October came what can only be described as the game of the season, we were at Pride Park Derby County for a league fixture, to be honest anybody would have thought it was an FA Cup tie, it was so exciting well perhaps not for the managers, especially their heart rates, it all began with Ipswich Town on fire, Berra and Murphy putting Town 0-2 up after only 9 minutes, only for Derby to score and make it 1-2 on 12 minutes, game on I hear you say! Well it certainly was a couple of minutes later as Creswell made it 1-3 after 14 minutes, it was crazy, absolutely crazy, then believe it or not Tunnicliffe made it 1-4 on 34 minutes to send our fans into raptures of delight, 1-4 at half time no way we weren't getting three points tonight, or were we? Well Derby must have had a stern talking to because they came out of the blocks firing and reduce the arrears on 47 minutes 2-4, further goals in the 61st minute and heartbreakingly on 87 minutes to make it 4-4 a game I will never forget, but we got one point for it, we threw it away hook, line and sinker everyone.!

As usual as we had been now for several seasons we were dropping points all over the place and the next few games were to produce three draws and a defeat, form that would be no good if we were to be heading for the top end of the division, that was for sure. The next ten games leading up to Christmas saw us win five, draw three and lose only twice, a good return of points going into the New Year, much needed for the boys. The FA Cup saw us draw Preston North End, a famous club from the past, a club I've always admired actually for their famous history, a club that always says football to me. We drew the first game 1-1 at Portman Road only to lose 3-2 at Deepdale with Garner getting a hat trick, Nouble and McGoldrick scoring for Town in which was a game littered with goals and yellow cards in the second half, at the end of it was another cup exit at the first attempt, it was all starting to get more than predictable 100%.

As we continued our league season in the New Year we were sitting nicely in sixth place, leading up to our home games against QPR and Millwall, we lost both 1-3 at home to QPR and 1-0 to Millwall, not the greatest starts to what we all hoped would be a successful end of the season. The next five games produced two wins and three draws, so we were back on track sitting in 8th position with fifteen games to go, not too bad at all really, Mick was doing a sterling job at the time considering everything he had to deal with, that was my opinion anyway! Over the next period of seven games we won four, drew none and lost three, that was Ipswich Town to a tee at the time we just couldn't consistently put a winning run together good enough to catapult us to those play off places! We drew then with Forest at home with Murphy getting a late equaliser after Forest had gone 0-1 up very early on, it was followed by a defeat at Blackburn Rovers 2-0, a game which put a real dent in our hopes. Our last six games produced three wins, one draw and two defeats, to finish ninth, on 68 points, only four points behind Brighton in sixth, those two defeats at Watford and Burnley in our last three games really cost us dearly, but all in all a decent performance over the season by everyone, a tad of improvement I felt which left us feeling a bit more optimistic for the following season I felt, a little piece of stability had been found we hoped!

51 - STABILITY PLEASE MICK!
2014-2015

Mr McCarthy was still being very active in the transfer market and this season we saw the likes of Bialkowski, Parr, Bru, Collinson, Sears, Ambrose, St Ledger and Noel Hunt join the club, with also a whole host of loans joining as well, notably Williams, Wood, Chaplow, Varney and Conor Sammon, unfortunately we lost the services of players like Cresswell to West Ham, it was a sign of the times at the time, but hey ho we have to just grin and bear it and get on with it. At least Norwich City were back in the Championship AGAIN so at least we had a derby to look forward to or did we!?

Of course these days football clubs are really only as good as their owners, or most of them if you know what I mean, now our owner Mr Evans was unfortunately always conspicuous by his absence, in fact I have never ever seen him with my own eyes at Portman Road FACT!! Unbelievable because I am at Portman Road nearly as much as I am anywhere!! Yes he had pumped money into the club at the beginning but now it was a different story, the manager was really feeding on scraps and it wasn't easy for Mick McCarthy, but like I said before he was doing an okay job considering the circumstances everyone. 2014/2015 was our thirteenth consecutive season in the Championship and after what was a decent season the one before, could we kick on and get to those play offs and hopefully fulfil our dreams and get back to our home, the Premier League, time would certainly tell folks!

The season kicked off with a home game versus Fulham, a team that would struggle most of the season, we won 2-1 with goals from Murphy and McGoldrick, a pair that were to go on and have a marvellous season, especially Murphy who was prolific all season long, the crowd of 17,218 was disappointing to say the least, a sign of the times. It was early season and of course the meant only one thing, the League Cup, we drew Crawley Town and a game which was littered with yellow cards was lost 1-0 (aet) to a goal conceded in the 111th minute, this just added to all our other embarrassing results in this competition we had had previously, we just knew it would happen, it always does these days, out we go.

So back to league action and we didn't have a great start in the first give games, yes we beat Fulham but the next four were only to bring two points, that was from away draws at Birmingham and Derby County, in the middle of that mini run we had a certain derby game against our old mates Norwich City, and it didn't go well either. It was in front of 25,245 fans and of course the Sky cameras as usual, it was a typical Ipswich vs Norwich game with yellow cards, a great atmosphere as usual, but unfortunately the wrong result, Norwich won 0-1 with a goal from Grabban, we all went home with our tails between our legs, it is never easy losing to THAT LOT but hey ho we've just got to get on with it whether we like it or not! September was here and the next seven games brought four wins and three draws we were firmly back on track in what was certainly going to be a very competitive league this season, we were sitting sixth after twelve games. I was more than happy with that start, 100% everyone.

As usual as every other season had been, results were very much up and down, but nowhere as bad as normal, we were staying right up there in the table with the very best of them. Right from early November we went on a great run right up until Christmas, from ten games we won eight and drew only two including wins over Wolves, Watford, Leeds, Middlesbrough, Brentford and Charlton, four of whom would finish the season in the top seven in the table!! Out of those games the one that always sticks in my mind was the game at Brentford, we had loads of fans there as always and we scored more or less straight from the kick off from Murphy, he added a second on 21 minutes and Anderson put us three up on the half hour, dreamland for the Town, the second half was filtering out for a 0-3 win, but then the game exploded, Brentford scored after 80 minutes to make it 1-3, then two minutes later Tommy Smith scored to make it 1-4, only for Brentford to get another goal on 90 minutes to make the final score 2-4, a great game and a Boxing Day treat for everyone.

The FA Cup was with us again and we drew again the Saints from Southampton, in front of 31,201 fans we gave a great account of ourselves and held them to a 1-1 draw with Darren Ambrose netting our goal, a replay at Portman Road was just what we deserved on the day. The replay in front of 27,923 at Ipswich was not to be our day, and we succumbed to a Long goal and went out again at the first time of asking, this was becoming far to repetitive for me especially as I have only been used to very good cup runs in the past, but I suppose I just have to put up with it, it is what it is as they say these days everyone. The next nine league games running up to Carrow Road for the derby, we again were very roller coaster in our form, we won four, drew one and lost four, not brilliant, but we went into the Norwich game sitting in third place, a great achievement by all the players and especially McCarthy who was working on a shoestring folks. The derby game which had Alex Neil now in charge at City was a very even game to be honest, but again Norwich especially in recent times always seem to have the upper hand, and goals from Johnson and Grabban again gave them the points, we had our fair share of chances especially from Sears, but again it wasn't to be we couldn't dwell on it, we must just get on with the rest of the season and finish as high as we possibly can.

Another couple of defeats followed the Norwich game, but then we won a couple on the trot, including that famous game at Vicarage Road, Watford where we won 0-1 with Chaplow getting a 90th minute winner in front of the Town fans packed in the away end, everyone including Chaplow went mental, it was a marvellous day, and a great three points, against a side that would eventually finish second in the league table, that put us back into sixth place, a position that was a must now for the Town, it had to be! Our last seven games produced three wins, two draws, which one was against Bournemouth who were soon to become the Champions and two defeats, it was enough to secure a playoff place in sixth place, and guess who we had to play, yes, you have guessed it, Norwich who finished third on 86 points, a local derby that will test the nerves of anybody 100%.

The first leg, which was at Portman Road was watched by 29,166, the atmosphere was electric as you could imagine, but again City scored the opener, a goal by Howson on 41 minutes, we had to respond and how we did, we equalised on the stroke of half time, a goal be Anderson, and I can still see him celebrating now, he jumped as high as a kite into the Ipswich Sky, he and every Town fans went absolutely mental, the game finished 1-1, but like I say we were still in the tie, that was the main priority, nothing gets won in the first leg, that is for sure. The less said about the second leg the better, we lost 3-1 (4-2 on agg), Berra got sent off, when surely he would have been better letting it go in, but that's easy for me or anyone else to say, I'm not blaming Berra, he had a great season as did the rest of the lads, we just came up short, but that's football everyone! For the record Tommy Smith scored for us and celebrated wildly, good on your Tommy, you are a legend mate, Championship again!

52 - ONE STEP FURTHER?
2015-2016

Considering everything that Mick McCarthy had to deal with, what was basically nothing, I personally thought he was doing an okay job, his football wasn't always the best but he had to work with the hand he was dealt everyone. After losing to that lot down the A140 in the Semi Finals of the playoffs 2015-2016 it was always going to be a season that we would hope just might be the one we got back to the Premier League. Mick was really still wheeling and dealing, but not doing too bad a job with it to be fair to the man, this season he brought in Knudsen, Pitman, Coke, Toure and Douglas and a few others mainly on frees apart from Knudsen who was undisclosed, the loans in consisted of Fraser, Maitland-Niles, Digby, Pringle and Feeney. Most of these deals were done obviously on the back of the sale of Tyrone Mings to Bournemouth for £8 million, a deal that at the time had to be done to enable Mick to get anyone through the door at all!

Mings was one of eighteen players to leave the club during the season. The season kicked off at Brentford a ground which we do okay at most of the time and we got a point out of a game we really should have taken three points from, we were 0-2 up with goals from Bru and Fraser, only for Brentford to score twice in the last few minutes, gutted to say the least, we followed it up with a 2-1 home win in the League Cup over Stevenage, Yorwerth and Tabb turning the game around after we had gone in 0-1 down from a Berra og, second round here we come, shock and amazement!! So a decent start to a season which to be honest no one really knew how it would go after that devastating defeat to Norwich in the playoffs. The next three league games were to produce 9 points with wins over Sheff Wed 2-1 at home, Burnley 2-0 at home and a very good win at Preston away 1-2, results that were to put us top of the league after four games with ten points gained, fantastic effort by everyone involved. The League Cup was back again and we drew Doncaster away, we went 1-0 down mid way through the first half and we all thought here we go again, but no, we equalised through Pitman on 58 minutes and the game went to extra time, where we scored three times in extra time to finally win the game 1-4. Town still undefeated in the season so far! Unfortunately that was not to last any longer as our next two league games were to end in defeats to Brighton at home and Reading away (2-3 and 5-1 respectively), I was at the Reading game and it was an awful day, especially after equalising so quickly after they went 1-0 up, it was all down hill after that. Our next game was at Leeds United, and we won 0-1 courtesy of a Smith goal after 32 minutes, always great to win at Elland Road because its never easy. The League Cup draw saw us up against Man Utd at Old Trafford and although we lost 3-0 we gave a good account of ourselves and really were still in the game up until Pereira made it 2-0 on 60 minutes, we conceded the third in injury time so we didn't disgrace ourselves at all, well done lads!

Back to the league and in our next six league games we never even got a win, we drew four and lost two, not the kind of form we needed at this stage of the season if we were going to challenge for the playoffs at the very least. We were now fourteenth in the table and a whole lot of work to be done, that was for sure. The games leading up to the New Year were absolutely vital and out of our eleven games up to New Year we won seven, drew two and only lost two, to Middlesbrough at home and Derby County at home, twenty three points out of thirty three to leave us in sixth place going into the New Year fixtures, a very good position indeed, we really got ourselves very much back into contention indeed.

January only means one thing and that is the third round of the FA Cup and again we had drawn Portsmouth, after a very good game at Portman Road which finished 2-2, we went off to Fratton Park only to lose 2-1. We were 2-0 down at half time, but Niles got a goal back to 2-1, but then we had Malarczyk sent off and that was that in a nutshell really, out of the cup, again so early it really hurts. Our mates from Leeds United were back in Town and we got off to an absolutely awful start going 0-1 down in the very first minute from Doukara, but after a very shaky start we grew into the game and equalised on 50 minutes through Chambers, the game was looking like finishing 1-1 but then up stepped Pitman to score in the 92nd minute, the ground was jumping, well apart from the Leeds fans that is (lol), we had won and jumped into fifth place, lovely jubbly everyone. From now we had to push on in the league, but being Ipswich we didn't and we lost four of our next six games to leave us in tenth place, with a whole load of work to do in the remaining fourteen games of the season.

Things looked a lot brighter after our next two games against Huddersfield away 0-1 and Forest home, 1-0, two wins and both goals scored by Pringle, six very welcome points indeed. Our next ten league games saw us win only once against Blackburn 2-0, Murphy getting both goals, we were eighth in the table and we were in that position for what seemed an eternity, not even two wins from our last two games against MK Dons 3-2 at home, and a 0-1 win at Derby on the last day could see us into the top six, we finished seventh, five points off Sheffield Wednesday, it's the Championship again next season everyone!!

53 - MONEY GETTING TIGHTER AND TIGHTER 2016-2017

Season 2016-2017 was always going to be the same as any other over the last few seasons, the purse strings were well and truly pulled on Mick McCarthy and he had to make the best of whatever he could. This season Murphy was sold to Newcastle for £3 million and another twelve went out of the door mainly on free transfers. In came Ward for £600,000, Webster swap deal, Moore, Best, Spence, Taylor, Rowe and Digby, we also made quite a few loan deals, the main ones being Grant, Lawrence, Williams, Huws, Diagouraga and Samuel it didn't look to me to be too bad a bit of business, time would tell though as usual everyone! But the only problem I had was where we were signing these players from and with all due respect I'd never really ever heard of clubs like Forest Green Rovers, Worthing and Macclesfield, but these were the types of clubs were now doing business with, oh god how the mighty were falling! It was all getting so depressing on a football front for fans of my generation who had seen so many lovely days, managers, great chairmen, great board members, great great fans and we still have them, we will never go away and desert the club and so it has proved every one of our fans are true heroes one hundred percent!

The club was deteriorating by the minute and it was so sad to see, gates were not what they were for obvious reasons, the ground and everything around it was becoming dirty and shabby due to neglect on a huge level, it was awful to see for the genuine supporters who really cared for their club, in a word it was all very SHAMEFUL. Moving on from all that and of course another season was upon us and it all started with a fifteenth consecutive season in the second tier of English football with a game against Barnsley our old friends from the play off final and what a start for our new boy from Spurs Grant Ward. McCarthy made a substitution or two at half time, bringing Grant and Ward on and what a double change that proved to be, Ward scored 30 seconds after coming on, only to be pegged back by Hourihane on 49 minutes 1-1. Ward then scored his second quickly followed by McGoldrick putting us 3-1 up with a penalty, back came Barnsley to make it 3-2 through Watkins, only for Ward to complete a fantastic hat trick on his debut with a low drive into the net, a fantastic debut for the new lad from Tottenham Hotspur.

Surely after that performance on the opening day a first round cup tie against Stevenage AT HOME wouldn't provide much of a problem WRONG, we lost 0-1 in front of a paltry 6,858 fans at Portman Road, to say that was embarrassing is an understatement, what on earth were we doing losing to Stevenage, could it get worse? Wait and see folks!

So after a great start to the season against Barnsley and a horrific cup defeat by Stevenage where do we go from here I here you say Well the next three league games produced two draws and a defeat at Brentford, the derby against Norwich City finished 1-1, with Knudsen scoring on 45 minutes after Jerome had put Norwich in front at Portman Road, again it always seems to happen now, going on to beat Norwich at this point in my supporting Ipswich Town lifetime seems like an age away now, so so sad everyone, the game was watched by 23,350 a very poor attendance for a derby game, but sadly a sign of the times right now. We sat in thirteenth place in the league after the derby game against Norwich and to be honest we never really moved away from that position much, right the way up until Christmas in fact on Boxing day we were in sixteenth place, in nineteen games up to Boxing day we had won six, drew five and lost eight, a long winter and spring was to be in front of us, I was fairly convinced about that everyone!! It was all so predictable at the time we would win one, then lose or draw one, that was how it was and highlighted when we played Bristol City 2-1 and three days later we lost 2-1 at QPR, that is exactly how it was now and whether we like it or not we had to just grin and bear it. The FA Cup saw us paired with Lincoln at home from the non-league, now you like I probably thought that was a gimme, not a chance, we were actually lucky to get a draw, we went 0-1 down after 7 minutes but we equalised through a very good Lawrence goal on 12 minutes only to go 1-2 down again in the 65th minute, it looked to the world like we were going out, but

AGAIN up stepped Lawrence and saved our bacon on 86 minutes, a goal that truly saved our face. The replay was on national television and of course they could smell a rat and it duly came to pass on the 90th minute mark when Arnold scored to send Sincil Bank into delirium, to be honest, no more than they deserved, we were totally awful from start to finish and got what we deserved NOTHING!! Out of a major cup competition AGAIN at the first hurdle, totally unacceptable and embarrassing to boot.

McCarthy certainly wasn't making many friends at this point if any folks! We followed that awful night up with a defeat at Huddersfield 2-0 and in the next twelve league games we won only once at Aston Villa with a goal by Huws, the other eleven saw us draw nine times and lose two, that left us in seventeenth position in the league and to be honest, struggling. We did pick up a bit in the next four games, we won three and only lost one, the best victory being against Newcastle Utd at home 3-1 when Huws got that superb goal to round the game off nicely, it was now a celebration of the great Sir Bobby Robson every time we played Newcastle Utd, and this day was to be hailed as Sir Bobby Robson day, a fantastic reminder of a great Ipswich Town and Newcastle Utd legend, I'm sure he wouldn't have minded Ipswich winning because to be totally honest, it was at Ipswich and Ipswich alone where he really made his name in English top flight football.

Thank you Sir Bobby, thank you for everything, may you always RIP, love Ipswich Town supporters. After the Newcastle Utd game we had three league games to play Rotherham and Forest away and Sheffield Wednesday at home and we lost all of them to finish sixteenth in the table, the lowest I could ever remember at the time, where on earth were we to go from here, I really couldn't answer that at this moment in time my dear fellow Town fans, I really couldn't.

54 - WHERE NOW FOR MICK McCARTHY
2017-2018

After a totally underwhelming season in 2016-2017, Mick McCarthy surely had to do some serious transactions in the market and he brought Garner and Waghorn in from Rangers and also Huws signed permanently along with Adeyemi also from Cardiff City, lesser signings in my opinion were Drinan and Cotter, we had four loan signings Celina, Iorfa, Connolly and Carter-Vickers all decent loan signings I thought to myself. Seventeen players went out, the most noticeable being Tommy Smith a great club servant and also Berra who had had a very good Town career in my opinion, I was sad to see him go, another interesting departure was Kieffer Moore to Barnsley for £750,000 a great deal considering he had done absolutely nothing at all for us, a total failure at Ipswich Town, but not everyone can just fall into place at a club, it certainly didn't work for Moore that was for sure everyone!

The season could not have started any better for Town, we kicked off with Birmingham at home and Garner was quick off the mark with the winner in the 50th minute in front of 18,153, we followed this up with wins against Barnsley away 1-2 with McGoldrick and Waghorn on target and also 3-4 away at Millwall a game in a million, we went 1-0 down after about 40 seconds only to equalise in the 4th minute by Garner, we then went 1-2 up courtesy of a Waghorn goal in the 34th minute, to be pegged back again in the 36th minute by Millwall 2-2, that was not that for the first half as Waghorn again put Town 2-3 in added time of the first half, the second half was more even but burst into life in the 80th minute when Millwall made it 3-3 through Elliott, damn I thought but it wasn't all over as Spence scored in the 88th minute to send myself and all the Town fans at the Den into delirium it was an astonishing game, won by Town and a great three points and a very happy journey home at night!

We then played Brentford at home and again Waghorn and Garner were on target in a 2-0 home win, 12 points out of 12 and sitting in second place in the table, HAPPY DAYS INDEED everyone!!

Unfortunately it was not to last and our next two league games were both defeats 0-2 at home to Fulham and a 2-1 loss at QPR we were still fourth but it knocked the shine off a bit of what was a very good start to the season, but we picked up again and two wins in the next three against Bolton 2-0 and Sunderland 5-2 had us in fifth place and looking steady for the season as a whole really, the Sunderland game saw five different scorers Waghorn, Spence, Celina, McGoldrick and Ward it was a brilliant performance on the night, a game to remember! In the League Cup we had gone to Luton and won very well 0-2 with a brace from McGoldrick, but sadly went out in round two 2-1 at Palace, another dismal cup exit folks!! The trouble with Town as we were at this particular time was you never really know what team was going to turn up from week to week, so it came as no real surprise when we lost our next three league against Bristol City 1-3, Sheff Utd 1-0 and Norwich City 0-1 courtesy of a Maddison 59th minute winner, the less said about that the better I think, it was played in front of 24,928 fans, a poor crowd for a local derby everyone. My next trip was to Burton Albion, a ground I hadn't been to up until now, it was small, nothing like I had been used to in my lifetime, but enjoyable at the same time. We went 1-0 down to a Turner goal, only to make it 1-1 through Waghorn on 66 minutes, then it was to become the Celina show, he scored the winner from a free kick after 89 minutes and then went and threw his shirt into the Town fans, he did get it back in the end though so all was okay for him to finish the game lol.

We had twelve games up until the New Year and we won four, drew three and lost five, it was the story of our season really, very much up and down and we reached Christmas in eleventh place, not too bad but not too good either everyone. We started the New Year with a 4-1 defeat at Fulham a game which Spence saw red in the 54th minute, we were 0-1 up at half time, but after the sending off Fulham scored four times without a reply in seven minutes, unbelievable BUT TRUE! The biggest pick me up you could have after that was an FA CUP tie at home against Sheff Utd, but no, we lost 0-1 in front of a mere 12,057 out we go AGAIN! Surely a match against Leeds Utd at home could put us back on track and what a game we saw that day to win it from Celina, it simply sailed into the net from 30 yards past Wiedwald a goal fitting to win any game, we won 1-0 and Leeds had O'Kane sent off, a fantastic game indeed.

We were eleventh in the table but just treading water if I'm being honest, we never really seemed to move anywhere because of our up and down form. Our next four games saw us win one, draw two and lost to Wolves at home so we went into the local derby at Norwich City in twelfth place, not ideal but it is what it is. The game at Norwich was a typical local derby, tense, scrappy at times, better in places but we were doing okay and keeping well in the game and in the 89th minute went 0-1 through Chambers, Town fans going mental thinking this was to be the first derby win since 2009, but no, Klose equalised in the 95th minute, unbelievable I know, but unfortunately true, we were all gobsmacked, absolutely gobsmacked everyone! 1-1 it finished and that was all on my birthday, for goodness sake, and Sir Bobby Robsons as well.

It was revealed after the game McCarthy had said something not really very nice about the Town fans, it was an action of his that was never to be forgotten and never really ever healed, it was to prove the beginning of the end for Mick McCarthy although we weren't to know it at the time everyone! In the proceeding ten games we won three, drew two and lost five, the last one of those ten games we beat Barnsley 1-0 at home with a goal by Knudsen in the 54th minute but after the match it was to be the end of McCarthys reign as Ipswich Town manager, he was sacked after 279 games in charge, it was in my opinion a real shame in the end as for the most part of his time at Ipswich he had kept us either in contention or thereabouts for a decent amount of time, with little, or no budget and for that I personally thank you Mick! Thank You!

So, Bryan Klug was put in caretaker charge and taking a club in twelfth place over he had nothing to lose really so he basically just had to steady the ship until the end of the season, his four games were against Forest, Aston Villa, Reading and Middlesbrough and he won one, drew one and lost two, not too different from McCarthy to be fair, but he did have a very good away win 0-4 at Reading, which is always a good place to win, I love beating Reading. I don't know why I just do everyone! So we finished the season in twelfth place, but at the end of the day we were at least still in the Championship, and hopefully something to build on for whoever was to take the managers job in the summer.

55 - A NEW ERA?? OF DOOM AND GLOOM 2018-2019

On the 16th September 2018 we were to lose one of our greatest ever players, Kevin Beattie. Kevin was a one off, an unbelievable footballer, and would have CERTAINLY won 100 caps for his country ENGLAND if it wasn't for a shocking amount of injuries; some of which he suffered because of the courageous way THE BEAT played the game.

Kevin R.I.P.

The fans all LOVED YOU PAL.

So Mick McCarthy was gone, now was that to be a good thing, only time would tell, everyone at the time and I remember it well, we were very pleased when we all heard that Mr Evans was about to appoint a young up and coming manager in Paul Hurst from Shrewsbury Town, a manager who had a decent reputation and had just been to a playoff finals with the Shrews, I remember I was on holiday that summer in Cornwall and I saw some Shrewsbury fans in Padstow and I asked them about Hurst and they told me they were absolutely gutted to lose him.

He was very active in the transfer market that summer and he signed a couple of his old boys in Nolan and Nsiala, he also got in Roberts, Edwards, Harrison, Jackson and Donacien, later followed by Collins and Judge, it was okay but most were from leagues below for goodness sake!! Loans included Walters, Chalobah, Edun, Graham and Pennington, at least some of these were at least from decent clubs at last folks!

It was the 4th August 2018 and everyone was kind of looking forward to this new era, Hurst had his own big flag in the North Stand and everything looked really rosy, especially after 5 minutes of his reign when Edwards headed Town in front 1-0 to Town and a great start for Hurst, don't worry it wasn't to last for long as Blackburn scored after 20 and 29 minutes to go in 1-2 up at half time. Ipswich to their credit kept going after the break and equalised in stoppage time through Edun, it finished 2-2 and Town got a point out of a game they could well have lost. Hursts next game saw us travel to Rotherham another of Hursts former clubs and we dominated the game for the most part but could not find a breakthrough, Rotherham United won it in the 90th minute through Michael Smith, a cruel blow for Town who had played very well in the game but 1 point from 6 was not really the perfect start, far from it.

The League Cup was upon us and my goodness did Hurst need a win, now Exeter away is not what you would call a hard fixture with all due respect, but Town always seem to know a way to make it seem like a game at Old Trafford. We went 0-1 up through Jackson on 37 mins, only to be pegged back on 64 minutes, 1-1 it finished, so off we went to penalties and Bishop and Chalobah missing from the spot, Hurst still WINLESS. We all wanted Hurst to succeed, but the next game at home to Villa was a game that you just don't want to go behind in and we did after 21 minutes 0-1, but to be fair we soon were back in it after 36 minutes with a goal by Chalobah 1-1, now the last thing Hurst needed was a player to be sent off, but that was the case when Edun received a second yellow card and got his marching orders, Town hung on really well in the second half to get a draw, not too bad considering everything that had gone on. Our next two games were both away to Derby (2-0) and Sheffield Wednesday (2-1) a game that Nsiala scored in then got sent off, oh my goodness what a nightmare and worse still we had accumulated only two points from the first fifteen, we were 24th in the league, an all time low for yours truly, I had NEVER EVER WITNESSED anything like this in my whole life everyone!!

Next up was Norwich City who like us hadn't started the season very well, it was a game that we played okay and took the lead in the 57th minute through Edwards only for Leitner to equalise for that lot down the road, it ended 1-1 a game in which Skuse got quite a bad knock. The next five games saw us win none, draw three and lose two, that was six points out of thirty three and sitting in twenty third place, absolutely awful! So off we went to Swansea

City the twelfth game in the league of Mr Hursts reign as manager and what a game it turned out to be everyone, Swansea made the perfect start a goal after 8 minutes courtesy of Donacien (og) then Ipswich scored twice in four minutes through Edwards and an own goal by Van der Hoorn to put us 1-2 up at the break, but in the second half a certain Celina equalised for Swansea on 79 minutes only for Chalobah to score the winner for Town in the 84th minute and give Hurst his first win as a Town manager, oh how he must have been relieved we all certainly were that was for sure folks! It still left us 23rd in the league and to make matters worse Norwich were improving all the time (uggh)! Our very next two league games against QPR (0-2) at home and Leeds Utd (2-0) away were to prove the last games Paul Hurst was to manage Ipswich Town FC, enough was enough, he had had fifteen (15) games in charge including the League Cup and had won one (1) a truly appalling record by anybody's standards and unfortunately he just had to go.

I certainly wanted him to succeed, but at the end of the day he was a failure, a catastrophic failure 100%. Bryan Klug was put in charge for the game at Millwall following Hurst's departure, with new manager Paul Lambert watching in the stands. To be honest nothing much changed as Town were beaten 3-0 and didn't even have a shot on target, these were bleak times to be an Ipswich fan indeed, we finished the game in 24th place and deservedly so I may add everyone, this was dross, complete and utter dross. The Preston game up next was to be Lamberts first proper game in charge, again we had the "Lambo" signs out and like always we thought maybe Paul Lambert was the one to get us going again, let's be honest, he couldn't do any worse than Hurst could he? His first game finished 1-1 with Sears putting us 1-0 up on 45 minutes via a penalty, only for Preston to equalise by Gallagher on 73 minutes, they then had their goalie sent off on 75 minutes, but survived to full time, unfortunately for us, a point first up for Lambert.

The next ten games leading up until New Years day we only won one game drawing two and losing seven, the win coming against Wigan at home, a goal by Sears on 67 minutes just papering over some enormous cracks I'm afraid, we were rock bottom and it would take an awful lot more than Paul Lambert to get us out of this that was for sure everyone! Next up was the FA Cup and a draw against Accrington Stanley, I went on the coach to Accrington, as I had never been there before, it was just as I had imagined it to be, cold, small, lovely people but more importantly a marquee for all of us to go and have a pint. I met Lawrenson, Alex Scott and the Football Focus team in there, it was a great atmosphere, Town and Accy fans mixing and getting on like a house on fire, truly brilliant it all was.

It was all good until the game kicked off and to be short and sweet, we lost 1-0 with a goal by Billy Kee in the 76th minute, another cup run had been and gone, omg, oh for a cup run eh folks! We did actually win a game the following week a 1-0 home win over Rotherham United with Keane getting his first for the Town, was this to be an upturn in form, what do you think everyone? In the last 19 games of the season we won two, drew seven and lost ten (10), the only salvation a last day win over Leeds Utd (3rd in the table) 3-2, apart from that a dreadful season which saw us finish bottom of the table with a record of P46 W5 D16 L25 GD -41 PTS 31. I had just watched my boyhood favourite football club Ipswich Town get relegated into the third tier of English football for the very first time in my life and at that time in 2019, I had been going for 55 years since I was 7 years old, third tier of English football, I had never heard of it, let alone watched it!! It certainly was going to be a long summer that was for sure everyone.

Number 6 – The Beat R.I.P

Colin with Kevins daughter at the unveiling of the
Kevin Beattie statue at Portman Road

Colin pictured with Allan Hunter at the unveiling of the
Kevin Beattie statue at Portman Road

56 - COVID END TO THE SEASON
2019-2020

Following relegation the previous season, this was to be the first season I would see my football club Ipswich Town in the third tier of English football, and I had been going since 1964, that is 54/55 seasons at that point in time, it was certainly not something I or anybody else of my generation or older was looking forward to during that pre-season that was for sure!! The only thing initially I was looking forward to was going to some new grounds and getting them ticked off my list as they say! The summer was long that year and it seemed an eternity until the fixtures came out, but when they did we found out we were going to Burton Albion away on the first day, a fixture I was looking forward to until the 1st of July when I became very ill following a heart attack I sustained whilst gardening at home.

I was taken to West Suffolk Hospital in Bury St Edmunds where I stayed overnight, and then the next day I was taken by Ambulance to Papworth Hospital where I stayed for 23 days, I eventually had my operation on the 18th July and came out on the 24th July feeling very, very weak and tired but so glad to go home with my dear wife Venetia xx. I was home about 10 days before the season kicked off, but I had no intention at all of going to the football, I just didn't want to for the first time in my whole life. I just wanted to get better and do it slowly but surely in my own way everyone! I would go back, I knew that but not until I was stronger and ready. I cannot comment on the games as I was not going this season, but Lambert got several players in, Holy, Norwood, Wilson, Vincent Young and Keane not bad signings at this level we thought, also we got Garbutt, Norris, Georgiou and Earl on loan, twenty players went out of the club and further 18 players went out on loan including Bialkowski.

So a lot of activity in the transfer market was this to prove good or bad, we would have to wait and see on that one folks! So like I said I was not going to the games at this point and I didn't like commenting on games I haven't seen so this will just be a run down of the season in general everyone!

We started off at Burton and got a favourable win there with Garbutt getting the winner on 11 minutes. Our next ten league games saw us win seven and draw three which put us top of the table, a great tonic for anyone especially if you hadn't been very well, thank you very much Town. The League Cup had seen us drawn against Luton away, and again we went out very early indeed with a 3-1 loss at Kenilworth Road, Dobra netting for Town. After our eleven game unbeaten start to the season you just knew we would probably lose somewhere like Accrington Stanley, and guess what we did 2-0, followed three days later by another defeat at home to Rotherham 0-2, we needed a boost and we got it from the next five games when we won two and drew three which left us still second in the table. In the FA Cup first round we got revenge on Lincoln after drawing 1-1 at home, we beat them at Sincil Bank 0-1 with Judge getting a late winner in the 94th minute, it was Coventry away in round two and after leading 0-1 we got pegged back and finished the game 1-1 so a replay at Portman Road only for Coventry to win 1-2 and put us out of another cup competition early, oh for the good old days I hear you all say.

The next five league games up until New Years day saw us win none, draw two and lose three, not promotion form at all but at least we were still fifth in the table and with a more than good chance of promotion. The next four games Accrington (4-1), Oxford away (0-0), Tranmere away (1-2) and Lincoln at home (1-0) saw us back on top of the table after 27 games and looking good, here's hoping everyone.

Just when I thought we had got it all going along very nicely, yes you have guessed it we lose three games out of the next four and drop right down to seventh place, totally unbelievable and even worse for myself having to listen to all of this on the radio just not the same, trust me everyone! The next six games saw us win one, draw one and lose four more which at the time after 36 games saw us positioned in tenth place, the season then was suspended due to the outbreak of Coronavirus, so our last fixtures of the season were curtailed. On the 9th June it was decided that the season would not continue and that all final league positions were to be decided on a points per game basis, that meant Ipswich Town would now drop to eleventh in the table, meaning it would be our worst finish in the Football League since the 1952-1953 season, a total embarrassment to everyone including myself who has ever supported the great Ipswich Town FC.

57 - ALL CHANGE AT THE CLUB
2020-2021

Covid 19 was still rife in the country, and football wasn't the same as we had all known it, no crowds, no atmosphere, watching iFollow, it was all so horrible only a true football fan could explain it to you, it just wasn't right at all, oh to have it back how it should be everyone!

Anyway a season of sorts had to be played and Lambert was not pulling up trees in the transfer market that was for sure, we brought in Cornell, Hawkins, Ward with McGuiness, Bennetts, Thomas, Harrop, Parrott and Matheson coming in on loan, we ousted Keane, Roberts, Rowe, Henderson and Cotter. I would like to say it was interesting but to be quite honest it wasn't apart from the fact we had got rid of Keane, injury prone yes, but on his day a match for anyone, especially in League One. In myself I was feeling a whole lot better and getting on with my life as much as I possibly could under the circumstances, it was very difficult as it had been for so many others, I certainly couldn't wait to get back to my second home Portman Road whenever that would be folks. Having said that I still didn't really 100% feel confident enough to go back to football as yet, but as Covid was still everywhere I wouldn't have been able to anyway! Clubs were still playing behind closed doors, well they were up till December, then the league decided to allow around 1,800-2000 into grounds, then it all struck again and we were behind closed doors again for basically the rest of the season.

The season itself started off very well under the circumstances, Lambert was still in charge and he was rather like marmite to me, you either liked him or you didn't, my take on him was I could put up with him, but I wouldn't go further than that everyone!

The first twelve games produced eight wins, one draw and three defeats, that was 25 points out of 36, good enough to see us in to third place in the league, very acceptable indeed, the next six games were to produce only two wins, one draw and three defeats, which saw us in fifth place in the league leading up to four consecutive games being postponed due to Covid, this really was an unprecedented time in football, nobody really ever knew whether they were coming or going to be honest folks. In the cups of '20-'21 we had done no better than normal, in the EFL Trophy we finished bottom and in the League Cup after beating Bristol Rovers 3-0 at home, we went out to Fulham 0-1 with a goal by Mitrovic, the FA Cup 1st round was no better we had a home draw against Portsmouth and lost 2-3 (aet) we were out of all competitions before Christmas unbelievable I hear you say, not really anymore.

By the New Year Lambert was coming under more and more pressure, although sitting eighth in the table we really needed wins and quite a few of them as well. In the eleven games leading up until Lamberts departure we won four, drew three and lost four, which although still had Town in eighth place in the league, the owner thought enough was enough and Paul Lambert was sacked, to be replaced by Mr Paul Cook with Matt Gill looking after matters in the meantime. Cook watched from the stands as we won our third game on the spin when we beat Accrington away 1-2 with goals from Wilson and Norwood, who also missed a penalty as well in the 19th minute, so Paul Cook took over at Ipswich with Town 7th in the league, and with still a very good chance of promotion, no pressure there then Mr Cook. His very first game in charge was against Gillingham away, we were still very much under the control of Covid 19 so no away fans to give Cook a good welcome to the club. It probably was a good thing for him because we lost 3-1 to a very average side, not the best start, but hey ho everybody deserves a chance or something like that, was this too big a club for him? Time certainly would tell everyone!

As everyone who knows myself knows, I absolutely love this football club and always have but under Mr Evans the club was slowly but surely becoming a disaster, as regards to the ground it was just getting worse and worse and everything was being left to deteriorate and it was awful to have to witness, even the astroturf what I always walked across to clean my dads plaque was old, horrible and totally neglected, it nearly made me cry every time I walked on it to be honest!! My club, our club was becoming a shambles, sorry correction had become a shambles and I hated it with a passion everyone, here was a club I had supported since 1964 and it was falling apart in front of my own eyes, it is and was totally devastating. The football we have all had to put up with in the past so many years had become stale, ordinary, pathetic at times, but we support the club and try our very best, I just wish sometimes other people had mine and your (fans) passion, we certainly would not be where we are now if that was the case, maybe I'm wrong, I don't know but that is what I think anyway. Yes I know Mr Evans has put millions in to the club, and I thank him HUGELY for that, but the money was spent unwisely by certain managers and we are where are, we will continue to follow our great club and hopefully be back to where we think we rightfully belong before very soon. I pray for that day and cannot wait for the younger supporters to feel a tad of success, my goodness they all deserve it 100%

Anyway, back to the here and now, and we still had a great chance of reaching the playoffs if we could find some kind of form at all we were still in eighth position and had a great outside chance, our next seven games saw us accumulate nine points out of twenty one, not brilliant by any means, but still had us believe it or not in eighth place, mad but true everyone! The last game of the seven was against Rochdale on the 5th April 2021, it ended 0-0 nothing new there then I hear you all say, but what was new was the fact although we didn't know it at the time it was to be the last game under the ownership of Mr Marcus Evans.

He sold up on April 7th 2021 to our new American owners Gamechanger 20 Ltd, to say I and every other Town fan was relieved would be an understatement it was time for a new era, one thing I would like to say about Mr Evans is this, yes he made mistakes, like any other businessman, but he did pay off an enormous debt to the club and for that I and every other Town fan should be extremely grateful for "thank you Marcus". So we had new owners, new chairman and CEO to come a bit later on it was all very exciting indeed and to listen to Brett, Berkay and Mark Detmer speak to us was music to our ears, the promises were on a different level, I just pray that they ALL get fulfilled especially for the youngsters. Anyhow we still had a season ongoing that potentially could still end with a promotion back to the Championship, we were still in eighth place in the league and with a real big push we could quite easily be in a playoff final at Wembley come May, or so we all hoped everyone!

We started off the new era with a home game versus MK Dons, it finished 0-0 in front of a crowd of nobody, but at least we had our new chairman of the board, a certain Mr Mike O'Leary a great football man and a very nice gentleman to boot, at last we were actually starting to build something concrete, a lovely feeling indeed. Our next game was against AFC Wimbledon and we got stuffed 3-0 admittedly getting Harrop sent off after 28 minutes didn't help, but it was awful, this was what Paul Cook had took on, could he handle it? I would like to think so and I was prepared to give him a bit of time, everyone deserves that I always think folks! It was around this time that I linked up with the Talking Town podcast after a chat with my friend Richard Moss, it is something I have NEVER regretted and have made loads of new friends through the channel, obviously Martin Lambert (Guv) and Matt Phillips are two that very much spring to mind, but there are loads of others and you all know who you are and I hope we all remain friends for ever and a day, and I mean that from my heart all of you. So we sat ninth with six games to go, now if you are serious about promotion, 9 points out of 18 isn't going to get you there, especially if your team is losing 3-0 to Northampton Town, yes, you heard it right Northampton Town, we finished ninth, NINTH IN THE THIRD DIVISION, things needed to change, and change quickly hopefully the new ownership and the new CEO could force this change, who knows everyone, here's hoping and praying folks.

Colin and ITFC Chairman Mike O'Leary at Lincoln

Mark Rattle, George Nunn, Colin pictured with one of the "Three Lions" Mark Steed, and new CEO Mark Ashton

Colin pictured with new CEO Mark Asthon

58 - COVID OVER (ISH) WELCOME MR ASHTON AND KIERAN McKENNA 2021-2022

Considering the previous season had been again nothing short of a disaster, I say disaster because ninth place in the old third division is simply not good enough, it might be for some, but for myself it wasn't anywhere near good enough, things certainly had to change and my goodness how they changed! Bearing in mind I have been going to Portman Road since 1964, I had watched Town from 1964-2019 ONLY in the two top divisions the first division (Premier League) or the second division now known as the Championship, that is 55 consecutive years of NOT being in the third tier, not a bad record everyone. So the last couple of seasons had been so new to me, going to stadiums that to be honest I really didn't think existed (lol), it was kind of surreal in a way. I think we all started to think when on earth is this all going to stop and we get back to where we belong, that certainly was my chain of thought anyway.

So the first change in the summer was the appointment of a new CEO and it was Mark Ashton from Championship Bristol City, now a lot of supporters from the Bristol area were saying this and that about Mr Ashton, but my opinion was this, I went to Ashton Gate in the '70s and '80s and it was an average first and second division ground at best, when Mr Asthon left Bristol City, the place was completely transformed on and off the pitch, the ground itself was and is superb, all thanks to their CEO, sour grapes I would suggest, I was more than happy to have him at Portman Road, that was for sure everyone! So on June 1st 2021 Mr Ashton was at last at his desk at Portman Road and what a summer we were in for, it was a transfer window like no other, I certainly hadn't seen anything like it in my entire life, it was bordering on unbelievable to say the very least.

Transfers in came to eighteen over the season, loans in came to seven, transfers out came to twenty six, and loans out came to twelve, that is what you call a lot of business over a season bordering on mental if you like. Of those transferred out we said goodbye to Chambers and Skuse both to Colchester Utd, now although probably not the most gifted players in the world I admit, they were fantastic club servants and we should only thank them for their services. I certainly did. Dozzell also departed for £1 million, good money considering how many times he played for Town, he had injuries yes, but a good deal in my opinion. Of the players brought in the ones who stood out for myself were Burns, Evans, Piggott, Fraser, Edmundson, Chaplin, Aluko, Morsy and Walton, the loans that stood out were Coulson, Bonne, Barry, Walton and obviously Bersant Celina who had made his return to Portman Road again, some of these players were to shine and others were very much a disappointment to say the least, I will let you all gauge who you thought was good and not so good everyone.

This up and coming season, especially after another disastrous placing in the league in 2020-2021 was in my opinion make or break for Paul Cook, I personally had nothing against the man, I wanted him to succeed just like any Ipswich Town manager, but with all that had gone on in the last couple of months I really was thinking oh my goodness, you have to hit the ground running here Paul Cook or face the consequences!! It really was win or bust!

So the season was here, we had new owners, a new Chairman, a new CEO, new players, new staff and over 21,000 excited fans back in the ground after COVID what could possibly go wrong everyone? We kicked off against Morecambe at home, a game which you would have thought would have been ideal for an opener, WRONG! It proved anything but ideal, in fact we were 0-1 down after 22 minutes, a goal scored by Stockton, a big powerful centre forward who would go on and have an excellent season by the way. We had loads of possession, in fact 67% to be exact and we finally equalised through Fraser who had played a clever one-two with Chaplin, surely we would go on and win from here, wrong again because Stockton had other ideas and scored his and Morecambe's second on 72 minutes after he had robbed Luke Woolfenden and rounded Hladky to put the ball away 1-2. We just had to get something from this first game and it duly came by substitute Bonne in the 91st minute, he latched onto a ball by Norwood and he made it 2-2, not an ideal result, but a draw is better than losing I suppose, plenty of work to be done up the training ground, that was for sure folks!!

The new owners were saying all of the right things when we got to hear from them over the various links in the media, it was certainly heaven, music to the ears to hear our owners being so positive, not only about the present, but more importantly about our future, so many ideas going forward, it really was becoming very exciting indeed, on top of this of course we had Ed Sheeran on board now as well, sponsoring the kits, it was a million miles away from where we had been over the last 13 years or so, it was a case of getting OUR CLUB back and that was basically all we ever wanted, thank you most sincerely to the owners, Chairman, CEO, Ed Sheeran and everyone else who has made this happen, you have made a lot of fans very happy indeed, now all we need to do is get out of this awful league we are in please!!

Following the Morecambe game we were back in League Cup action and trust me that didn't last long we drew Newport County at home. Now normally that would more or less be a simple task of putting us through into round two WRONG! We lost 0-1 with Newport scoring in the fourth minute and try as we might we just couldn't break them down, out we go again, embarrassing totally embarrassing everyone! So it was back to the league and we must get wins and get our confidence going for what was surely going to be an awkward season if we didn't watch out. Burton Albion away was next and we just don't learn our lessons at all in the league, we went 1-0 down after 19 minutes and even an own goal by O'Connor of Burton to make it 1-1 didn't stir us to any great extent, we did get a penalty after Barry was brought down, only for Fraser to see his penalty saved by Garratt and then just as we thought we had got a point, Burton got themselves a penalty when Penney produced a foul on Powell up stepped Atkins to fire home in the 86th minute, disaster, one point out of six from two winnable games, not the start Cook or the brilliant Town fans wanted 100%, must do better!

The very next game was away against Cheltenham, with me still being on holiday from my job at the school it was perfect timing for myself to do yet another away day at a venue I had never been to before, I used to always think Cheltenham was only for race goers obviously not. I went on the coach for a change, it was not the best of journeys as one of the other buses kept breaking down, we eventually got to Cheltenham at 19:15pm, so we made kick off phew! The game itself was very good in the first half, we went in front with a strike by Penney and could and should have been 0-2 up when Bonne missed an absolute sitter, was that to cost us, you bet it was folks. Town were still in command after the break but we couldn't get that second, Cheltenham took advantage and equalised on 62 mins with a goal by Wright, we succumbed again to ANOTHER long throw when Boyle scored at the far post, another game without registering a win, just not good enough at all. At least our next three games were at home to MK Dons, AFC Wimbledon and Bolton Wanderers, games surely we were going to pick up wins and climb that table, sadly no, we drew two of them 2-2 and lost very embarrassingly 2-5 at home to Bolton, a game Walton was making his debut, oh what a shocker it was for him and us fans, we had taken three points out of eighteen, seriously shocking! Things must change and soon, this is third division football for goodness sake everyone!! We were again involved in that EFL Trophy and after losing at home to West Ham U21s 1-2, we beat Gillingham away 0-2 and drew 0-0 at home to Colchester United, winning 4-3 on pens, we eventually went out 3-4 on pens to Arsenal U21s after drawing the game 2-2, a god send in my opinion to be out of a competition that most people feel is meaningless, especially when a club like Ipswich is mainly focussed on promotion or at least should be. It was so lovely to be able to travel to games again and our next game was Lincoln away, I drove to this one and again Town fans sold out the away end, totally unbelievable considering our start to the season, again this was yet another away ground ticked off my list.

I met up with, and sat with friends of mine from Talking Town, Richard, and boys, Kally, TJ etc. it really was an enjoyable day. Town played well on the day and won it with a goal from Bonne after 30 minutes. Second half was a bit edgy at times but we had done enough for the three points, after the game Mr Ashton came bombing down to the away end and was high fiving everyone, he even gave bear hugs to myself and Rich it was a truly brilliant away day, Town had won a game eventually, and also a big shout out to Mr O'Leary the Chairman who I met before the game, a true gentleman, and we are so lucky to have him on board.

The very next game against Sheffield Wednesday will always be remembered for Bonne pinching the ball off Peacock-Farrell and eventually Chaplin scoring in the 90th minute after Bonne had done so well, we had earlier gone 0-1 down, so a point off a good Wednesday side was more than acceptable. Doncaster at home next, so we move on as they say. The Donny game was a mauling to say the least, we won 6-0 and it could and should have been double figures, Evans got a well deserved hat trick, Bonne scored twice and Edmunson also netted, a great night for everyone, players, fans alike hopefully the tide had turned or had it? Well we soon found out next up was Accrinton away, Bonne again put us 0-1 up only for Accy to storm back in the second half and goals by Bishop and Pell saw us back to square one, so disappointing especially after the last couple of games, we just need to find consistency, simple as. Well I thought that we had to a greater extent because in our next 6 games we won four, drew one and lost only one, we beat Shrewsbury, Portsmouth, Fleetwood and Wycombe, two of those being at Fratton Park and Wycombe scoring four on both occasions, surely the tide had well and truly turned for Mr Cook, or had it? To be honest we had been playing some decent stuff, no more so than at Portsmouth, a game I went to and also at Wycombe but we were still only ninth in the table, not bad for some, but certainly not good enough for Ipswich Town.

The next four games, Oxford at home, draw, Sunderland and Rotheram both defeats and ironically a win at home to Crewe was to see the end of Paul Cook, he was sacked on 4th December

2021 to be replaced by John McGreal as caretaker manager, he would be in charge for the forthcoming game at Charlton with Dyer assisting him for the time being until another manager was appointed. A dismal display at Charlton where we never had a shot on target, eventually losing 2-0 and a brave performance at Wigan where super sub Norwood earned us a very creditable 1-1 draw were to be the last couple of games before we appointed Mr Kieran McKenna as our new manager on 16th December 2021, here was a very young up and coming coach from Man Utd who wanted to be his own man, confidence in his own ability and a very nice gentleman to boot, he comes with my blessing and thousands of others it reminded me so much of when we appointed a fresh faced Sir Bobby Robson from Fulham all those years ago, and Kieran was exactly the same age as Bobby was, now there's a coincidence for you all everyone "good luck" Kieran from all Town fans everywhere. His first game was Sunderland at home, and what a day that was, we had 29,005 in the stadium, Kieran McKenna watched from the stands that day as Town roared on by a loud crowd went in front on half time with a goal by Norwood. Sunderland came back and levelled on 50 minutes, but Town were by far the better side but couldn't get that winner, 19 shots to Sunderlands 5 tells their own story, but again we had to settle for a point, so often the end of the story unfortunately everyone. So here we were after 23 games and still eleventh in the table, shocking really!

Prior to the Sunderland game we had another crack at trying to at least get to the third round of the FA Cup, a round that I had only known as I was growing up and also as a young and older man, this first round stuff for me was only for non league teams and also rans of the Football League, with all due respect to them of course! We played Oldham in the first round and knocked them out 1-2 at their place after an awful game at Portman Road in front of 8,845 fans, the second round saw us draw with Barrow at home 0-0 in front of 6,425 a shocking attendance, so off we went to Barrow in front of 2,756 supporters and also live TV cameras, I wonder why they were there, yes to see an upset and quite honestly how we played it was not an upset more a comfortable night for Barrow FC who went through deservedly 2-0 on the night, how much lower could we go folks? So it was back to league action under Kieran McKenna and to be honest there was a change in our way of playing and also our attitude towards most things which was a joy to see but results first and foremost was what everyone really needed and wanted.

Our next ten games saw us win seven times, draw one and lost two, not a bad return really which saw us up to ninth place with more than a chance if we kept it going. Out of those ten games of which six were away, I went to Gillingham 0-4 fantastic performance, Sheffield Wed 1-0, where we ought to have at least got a draw and MK Dons of which we took 7,000 fans to ground where the attendance was only 15,311, they said they had just a few more in the ground than us, I would question that I think we had more, in fact I know we had more, 10,000 next season please MK Dons, we would sell them, don't worry about that anyone. Our very next game was Burton Albion at home, a very significant game for myself as it was my granddaughter Alice's first game at Portman Road, it was pouring with rain bless her but it couldn't stop her seeing her first goal at Portman Road after 49 seconds of the game, surely another record for the Plumb family, it was so surreal, we finally ended up winning 3-0, so a great birthday present for yours truly, we were still ninth something that seemed to be set in stone in this season of ours everyone. Wins and lots of them were what was needed and in our next seven games we won three, drew four and lost none not bad but we were drawing just too many games. The last of the seven games was against Plymouth at home and it was a celebration of the life of our great centre forward Paul Mariner, a legend of the club folks. Blue Action put on a fantastic show that day and should be highly commended for their display, it was emotional but also very nice indeed, well done lads, we also won 1-0 on the day a perfect way to end a really superb weekend. By this time of the season games were running out and we were still ninth, yes still ninth so in the last six league games we really needed to win them all to have any remote chance of making the playoffs a tall order I know but hopefully possible? How wrong I was, everyone. We started off with a shocking performance against Cambridge Utd with a 0-1 home defeat in front of 26,515 fans, quite remarkable considering we were still ninth in league one for goodness sake. We then played Shrewsbury away a game I went to and sat next to my friend Matt Stannard and his wife Caz, and his boys Archie and Hughie, we drew 1-1 with Norwood scoring after 6 minutes, we really should have buried them in the first half, but didn't it surely was all over for Town now as regards the playoffs, that's what I thought anyway.

Another away day followed for myself, a 1-0 defeat at Rotherham United, it was all over another season in League One beckoned folks, not something I or anyone else needed, but hey ho that's reality Colin. I didn't go to Wigan 2-2 away, but I did travel to Crewe and again sat with the Stannard's always a treat to see and sit with Hughie and Archie, Caz and Matt, it was a typical end of the season game ending 1-1 with Chaplin netting for Town. We finished off the season with an emphatic 4-0 win over Charlton with Bakinson, Burns (2) and Norwood on the scoresheet, it was played in front of 26,002 fans, a truly remarkable attendance considering we finished eleventh in the old third division, well done to everyone who has and continues to support our great football club, you are simply amazing ALL OF YOU.

Are there signs of encouragement under Mr McKenna YES THERE ARE, but we need to hit the ground running in 2022-2023 and get out of this awful league that we are in, do I think we will? YES I DO and the sooner the better and then I can continue to SUPPORT our club in the top two leagues, that I have only ever known in most of my 58 years of supporting the club I love and always CONTINUE to love COME ON KIERAN you can do it, I know that you can (Colin) x

Colin pictured with new manager Kieran McKenna

Colin and "Hockz" at Cheltenham

Paul Cook and "The Fisherman"

Lee Bayliss, Colin and Stephen Parry at Morecambe

Colin, Mark Rattle and his sons at Accrington

Peter Cox and Martin "The Guv" Lambert at Cambridge

Diary of an Obsession   240

Neil Perks, Matt Stannard and Colin at Plymouth

Caz, Archie and Hughie and Colins Flag at Crewe

RIP – Paul Mariner – Number 9

Colin with Luke Woolfenden at Portman Road

Colin with Sone Aluko at Portman Road

Paul Cook, Richard Moss and the late Martin Swallow (R.I.P)

Neil, Amber and Colin visiting Portman Road
from the South West

Portrait of Sir Bobby Robson, given to Colin on his birthday
(same day as Bobbys) by Sarah and Stephen Davies

Diary of an Obsession   244

MY TOP 100 PLAYERS

* = Players who represented their country while at Ipswich Town

Aaron Cresswell
Alan Brazil *
Alan Lee *
Alex Bruce *
Alex Mathie
Allan Hunter *
Arnold Muhren *
Bartosz Bialkowski
Bersant Celina *
Billy Baxter
Bobby Petta
Boncho Genchev *
Brian Talbot *
Bryan Hamilton *
Carlos Edwards *
Chris Kiwomya
Claus Thomsen *
Clive Woods
Cole Skuse
Colin Harper
Colin Viljoen
Craig Forrest *
Cristophe Berra *
Danny Haynes
Danny Hegan
Darren Bent
Daryl Murphy *
David Best
David Johnson (1st) *
David Linighan
David Lowe
David McGoldrick *
David Wright
Eric Gates *
Fabian Wilnis
Frank Brogan
Frank Yallop *
Frans Thijssen *

Gareth McAuley
Gavin Johnson
George Burley *
Geraint Williams
Gerry Baker
Gus Uhlenbeek
Herman
Hreidarsson *
Ian Collard
Ian Cranson
James Scowcroft
Jamie Clapham
Jason De Vos *
Jason Dozzell
Jermaine Wright
Jim Magilton *
Joe Broadfoot
John McGreal
John O'Rourke
John Wark *
Jon Walters *
Jonas Knudsen *
Kelvin Davis
Kevin Beattie *
Kevin Wilson *
Kieron Dyer
Laurie Sivell
Luke Chambers
Luke Woolfenden
Marcus Stewart
Richard Wright *
Roger Osborne
Romeo Zondervan
Russell Osman *
Shefki Kuqi *
Mark Brennan
Mark Venus
Martijn Reuser
Matt Holland *
Mauricio Tarrico

Mick McNeil
Mick Mills *
Mick Stockwell
Neil Thompson
Owen Garven
Pablo Counago
Paul Cooper
Paul Mariner *
Paul Mason
Peter Morris
Ray Crawford *
Richard Naylor
Simon Milton
Steve McCall
Steve Whitton
Terry Butcher *
Tommy Carroll *
Tommy Miller
Tommy Smith *
Tony Mowbray
Trevor Putney
Trevor Whymark *
Wes Burns *

EUROPEAN QUALIFICATION OR TROPHIES IPSWICH TOWN HAVE WON IN MY LIFETIME

* = TROPHIES OR COMPETITIONS I SAW IPSWICH TOWN PLAY IN OR WIN

DIVISION 3 CHAMPIONS	1956-1957
DIVISION 2 CHAMPIONS	1960-1961
DIVISION 1 CHAMPIONS	1961-1962
DIVISION 2 CHAMPIONS *	1967-1968
TEXACO CUP WINNERS *	1972-1973
FOOTBALL COMBINATION WINNERS *	1972-1973
FA YOUTH CUP WINNERS *	1972-1973
FA YOUTH CUP WINNERS *	1974-1975
FOOTBALL COMBINATION WINNERS *	1975-1976
FA CUP WINNERS *	1977-1978
DIVISION 2 CHAMPIONS *	1991-1992
PLAY OFF WINNERS (1ST DIV) *	1999-2000
PREMIER LEAGUE RESERVE WINNERS *	2001-2002
FA YOUTH CUP WINNERS *	2004-2005

EUROPEAN QUALIFICATION OR TROPHIES IPSWICH TOWN HAVE WON IN MY LIFETIME

UEFA CUP WINNERS *	1980-1981
WE QUALIFIED FOR THE EUROPEAN CUP	1962-1963
WE QUALIFIED FOR THE UEFA CUP *	1973-1974
WE QUALIFIED FOR THE UEFA CUP *	1974-1975
WE QUALIFIED FOR THE UEFA CUP *	1975-1976
WE QUALIFIED FOR THE UEFA CUP *	1977-1978
WE QUALIFIED FOR THE CUP WINNERS CUP *	1978-1979
WE QUALIFIED FOR THE UEFA CUP *	1979-1980
WE QUALIFIED FOR THE UEFA CUP *	1980-1981
WE QUALIFIED FOR THE UEFA CUP *	1981-1982
WE QUALIFIED FOR THE UEFA CUP *	2001-2002
WE QUALIFIED FOR THE UEFA CUP *	2002-2003

I didn't miss a European home game between when we played Real Madrid (1973) and the last time we played in the UEFA Cup in 2003.

GROUNDS I HAVE VISITED

1	Accrington	56	Man City (Old)
2	AFC Wimbledon (Old)	57	Man Utd
3	Amsterdam	58	Middlesbrough (Old)
4	Arsenal (Old)	59	Millwall (New)
5	Aston Villa	60	Millwall (Old)
6	Birmingham	61	MK Dons
7	Bristol City	62	Morecambe
8	Blackburn	63	Newcastle
9	Blackpool	64	Northampton (Old)
10	Bolton (New)	65	Norwich
11	Bolton (Old)	66	Notts County
12	Bournemouth	67	Notts Forest
13	Bracknell	68	Old Wembley
14	Bradford	70	Oldham
15	Brentford (Old)	71	Oxford (New)
16	Brighton (New)	72	Oxford (Old)
17	Brighton (Old)	73	Peterborough Utd
18	Bristol Rovers (New)	74	Plymouth
19	Bristol Rovers (Old)	75	Port Vale
20	Bruges	76	Portsmouth
21	Burnley	77	Preston
22	Burton	78	QPR
23	Cambridge	79	Reading (New)
24	Cardiff (Old)	80	Reading (Old)
25	Carlisle	81	Rochdale
26	Charlton	82	Rotherham (New)
27	Chelmsford	83	Rotherham (Old)
28	Chelsea	84	Scunthorpe
29	Cheltenham	85	Sheffield Utd
30	Chester	86	Sheffield Wednesday
31	Colchester United (Old)	87	Shrewsbury (New)
32	Coventry (Old)	88	Shrewsbury (Old)
33	Crewe	89	Southampton (New)
34	Crystal Palace	90	Southampton (Old)
35	Dagenham & Redbridge	91	Southend
36	Derby County (New)	92	St Etienne
37	Derby County (Old)	93	Stockport
38	Doncaster (Old)	94	Stoke (Old)
39	Everton	95	Sunderland (New)
40	Exeter	96	Sunderland (Old)
41	Forest Green Rovers	97	Swansea (Old)
42	Fulham	98	Swindon
43	Gillingham	99	Torquay
44	Grimsby	100	Tottenham Hotspur
45	Huddersfield (New)	101	Tranmere
46	Huddersfield (Old)	102	Walsall
47	Hull (Old)	103	Watford
48	Inter Milan	104	WBA
49	Ipswich	105	West Ham Utd (Old)
50	Leeds United	106	Wigan (New)
51	Leicester (Old)	107	Wolves
52	Leyton Orient	108	Wrexham
53	Lincoln	109	Wycombe Wanderers
54	Liverpool	110	Yeovil
55	Luton		

COLINS FAVOURITE....

FAVOURITE GROUNDS
PORTMAN ROAD, HILLSBOROUGH, OLD TRAFFORD

FAVOURITE MATCH
ST ETIENNE (AWAY) 1-4

FAVOURITE PLAYERS (ITFC)
KEVIN BEATTIE, JOHN WARK, PAUL MARINER, RAY CRAWFORD, MICK MILLS, COLIN VILJOEN, ARNOLD MUHREN, FRANS THIJSSEN

FAVOURITE GOAL (ITFC)
CLIVE WOODS vs LEEDS UNITED (FA Cup 6th Round 3rd Replay)

FAVOURITE GOAL (OPPOSITION)
LEIGHTON BAINES (WIGAN) (2004)

BEST BRITISH PLAYER SEEN AT PORTMAN ROAD
GEORGE BEST

BEST FOREIGN PLAYER SEEN AT PORTMAN ROAD
JOHAN CRUYFF

BEST INDIVIDUAL PERFORMANCE SEEN
IPSWICH 5 vs SOUTHAMPTON 2 (BRAZIL 5 1982)

WORST PERFORMANCE SEEN
MAN UTD 9 vs IPSWICH 0 (OLD TRAFFORD 1995)
PETERBOROUGH 7 vs IPSWICH 1 (LONDON ROAD 2011)

BEST PERFORMANCE SEEN
IPSWICH 7 vs SOUTHAMPTON 0 (1974)
IPSWICH 7 vs WBA 0 (1976-1977)
IPSWICH 6 vs MAN UTD 0 (1979-1980)

FAVOURITE OPPOSITION MANAGER
BRIAN CLOUGH (RIP) DERBY, NOTTS FOREST, BRIGHTON, LEEDS

FAVOURITE OPPOSITION PLAYER
COLIN BELL (MAN CITY) (RIP)

COLINS FAVOURITE….

WORST MOMENT AS A TOWN FAN
LOSING THE FA CUP SMI FINAL REPLAY AGAINST WEST HAM AT STAMFORD BRIDGE (1975)
LOSING TO AN AVERAGE MAN CITY IN THE SEMI FINAL AT VILLA PARK (1981)

BEST MOMENT AS A TOWN FAN
BEING AT WEMBLEY STADIUM WHEN WE WON THE FA CUP (1978)
BEING IN AMSTERDAM TO SEE THE TOWN LIFT THE UEFA CUP

MOST BIZARRE GAME WATCHED
BRISTOL ROVERS (AWAY) FA CUP - ABSOLUTELY ATROCIOUS ICE + SNOW

BIGGEST DISAPPOINTMENT
NOT WINNING THE TOP FLIGHT TITLE IN MY TIME ESPECIALLY IN 1981 BECAUSE WE WERE THE BEST TEAM IN EUROPE VOTED BY UEFA THAT SUMMER

BEST LOCAL DERBY WINS
IPSWICH 2 vs NORWICH 1 TEXACO CUP
NORWICH 1 vs IPSWICH 2 FINAL 1973
IPSWICH 5 vs NORWICH 0 FEB 1998

FAVOURITE AWAY FANS
NEWCASTLE UNITED (THERE'S ONLY ONE BOBBY ROBSON)

FUNNIEST MOMENT
ROBERT ULLATHORNE OG (IPSWICH vs NORWICH 1996)

FAVOURITE PRE MATCH MEAL
PIE AND A PINT

FAVOURITE SUPPORTERS IN GENERAL
OUR LOT (IPSWICH TOWN)

FAVOURITE TOWN FANS
MY DAD (RIP), MY BOYS (IAN AND ANDREW)
THE TALKING TOWN PODCAST TEAM

TEAMS IN EUROPE I HAVE WATCHED IPSWICH TOWN PLAY IN THE UEFA AND CUP WINNERS

1	REAL MADRID
2	LAZIO
3	FC TWENTE
4	LOKOMOTIVE LEIPZIG
5	FEYENOORD
6	FC BRUGES
7	LANDSKONA BOIS
8	LAS PALMAS
9	BARCELONA
10	AZ67 ALKMAAR
11	S.W. INNSBRUCK
12	SKEIDOSLO
13	GRASSHOPERS ZURICH
14	ARIS SALONIKA
15	BOHEMIANS PRAGUE
16	WIDZEN LODZ
17	ST ETIENNE
18	FC COLOGNE
19	ABERDEEN
20	ROMA
21	TORPEDO MOSCOW
22	HELSINBORG
23	INTER MILAN
24	AVENIR BEGGEN
25	FK SMEDEREVO
26	SLOVAN LIBEREC

I NEVER MISSED A EUROPEAN MATCH AT HOME FROM 1973-1974 UNTIL 2002-2003

We also faced Floriana FC and AC Milan in the European Cup but I was too young to go at the time.

NEVER LOST AT HOME

European Cup - All

P	W	D	L	F	A
4	3	0	1	16	5

European Cup - Home

P	W	D	L	F	A
2	2	0	0	12	1

Cup Winners Cup - All

P	W	D	L	F	A
6	3	2	1	6	3

Cup Winners Cup - Home

P	W	D	L	F	A
3	3	0	0	5	1

UEFA Cup - All

P	W	D	L	F	A
52	30	10	12	98	53

UEFA - Home

P	W	D	L	F	A
26	20	6	0	67	11

Total in Europe - All

P	W	D	L	F	A
62	36	12	14	120	61

Total in Europe - Home

P	W	D	L	F	A
31	25	6	0	84	13

Printed in Great Britain
by Amazon

19487885R00147